rare finds

A GUIDE TO BOOK COLLECTING

DAVID AND NATALIE BAUMAN

rare finds

Table of Contents

WHY COLLECT RARE BOOKS?   3

ON COLLECTING

    AMERICANA   7

    LITERATURE   17

    TRAVEL AND EXPLORATION   27

    CHILDREN'S CLASSICS   33

    SCIENCE AND NATURAL HISTORY   39

    MEDICINE   42

    ARTISTS' BOOKS   44

    PHOTOGRAPHY   46

    HISTORY   49

    ARCHITECTURE   53

    PHILOSOPHY AND LAW   57

    ECONOMICS   60

    RELIGION   63

    SPORT   66

    MUSIC   68

FORMAT   72

BOOK PRODUCTION   74

FREQUENTLY ASKED QUESTIONS   76

LIST OF REFERENCES   85

TYPES OF BINDINGS   92

GLOSSARY   98

ACKNOWLEDGEMENTS   104

"Words are all we have." Samuel Beckett

Why Collect Rare Books?

Why collect rare books? Because as you hold in your hands the first edition of any great book you hold something of its history, that moment when it was first presented to the world, new, original, without commentary or judgment. And in the book you hold you can acknowledge the trials it survived, everything from intentional destruction through censorship and burnings to the more mundane years of handling and simple neglect.

With every great first edition comes a story—the creative effort that propelled it into being, the practical negotiations that brought it into print, the popular reaction that brought it immediate fame or consigned it to obscurity for a time. A rare book collector knows that story and appreciates all of the book's struggles and successes. The pleasure of rare book collecting lies not only in each book's impact on the world and our own lives, but in our understanding of the random chances that produced it and allowed it to survive.

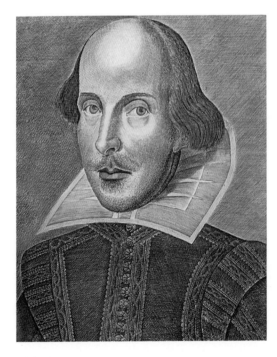

From the 1685 Fourth Folio:
engraved frontispiece portrait
of Shakespeare by Droeshout

INTRODUCTION

Something Really Happened

The anthropologist Claude Leví-Strauss wrote, "Objects are what matter. Only they carry the evidence that throughout the centuries, something really happened among human beings."

Objects—including and especially books—can matter. They testify that something really happened…

When Isaac Newton made his conceptual breakthrough (whether or not that apple fell on his head) and proposed the laws of physical motion in his *Principia Mathematica*…

When a slim, anonymous pamphlet, a mere "46 sheets," came off a Philadelphia press on January 10, 1776, exhorting readers to exercise *Common Sense* and fight for independence…

When the naturalist aboard the *H.M.S. Beagle* began formulating theories of natural selection that, when first published in 1859, immediately challenged accepted wisdom *On the Origin of Species*…

When Walt Whitman set ten pages of two-column, close-set type, part of what he called the "rough and ragged thicket" of pages that made up the first edition of *Leaves of Grass*…

When readers smuggled the earliest copies of James Joyce's *Ulysses*, bound in their iconic blue paper wrappers, into England and America, knowing that—whatever the moral authorities of the day said—they had found a revolutionary book…

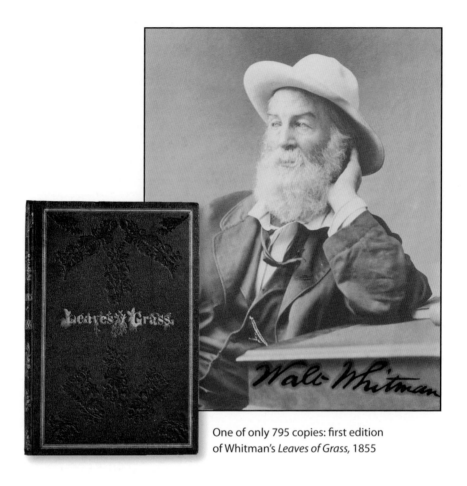

One of only 795 copies: first edition
of Whitman's *Leaves of Grass*, 1855

Something really happened... and books don't let us forget it.

Part of what's happening is *connection*. Books connect us to people whose ideas and achievements have shaped society. They link us to moments in which the world forever changed. Mark Twain's own copy of *Huckleberry Finn*... a worn copy of Patrick Gass' *Journal*, giving the world a first-hand account of the Lewis and Clark expedition... the 1953 issues of *Nature* announcing Crick and Watson's discovery of the double helix: to hold such pieces of history is to touch some of the outstanding intellectual, political, artistic and literary artifacts of the last six hundred years. Rare book collectors know that, in the books they own, something really happened—and their collections honor and preserve that human happening, now and into the future. To collect books is to celebrate the distinctive mark that human beings make on the world.

"I cannot live without books." *Thomas Jefferson*

What To Collect?

The decision about what to collect is a very personal one. The most important guideline is to collect whatever inspires you. There are numerous ways to design a collection. You can decide on a very narrow focus—such as authors' first novels, or the first editions of each title in a single author's career. Or you might seek the great works in a specific subject area, such as Americana, mathematics, history, or children's literature. You might collect great printing productions—artists' books, fine bindings, the great plate books. To follow is a selection of short essays on some specific subject areas that have become increasingly significant to collectors.

AMERICANA

From the earliest voyages of discovery to the founding of the new nation, from the exploration of the West to the turmoil of the Civil War, Americana is among the most compelling areas of collecting.

The American Revolution was fought in the press long before any shots were fired on the battlefield, and public debate about liberty continued well after independence was declared. First published in Philadelphia in January of 1776, Thomas Paine's *Common Sense* became the most widely read publication in America; Washington himself

First edition in English of Jefferson's
Notes on the State of Virginia, 1787

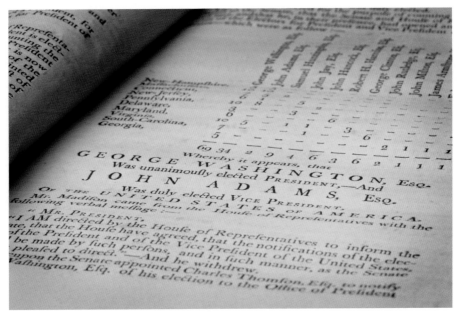

First printing of the first session of the Senate, 1789, containing one of the earliest printings of the Bill of Rights

commented, "I find *Common Sense* is working a powerful change in the minds of many." While the first edition is now virtually unobtainable, other 1776 printings are acquirable and important.

Numerous pamphlets chronicle the debates and decisions of the Continental Congress. Of course, the Congress' greatest legacy is the Declaration of Independence, drafted by Thomas Jefferson in 1776. All of the earliest printings of the Declaration are extraordinarily rare and valuable. But what of the political and philosophical works that influenced not only Jefferson, but Adams, Franklin, Washington and the other founders? The answer to this question leads many collectors to the first editions of Locke, Hobbes, Rousseau, Montesquieu and other philosophers whose books graced the shelves of colonial America.

When delegates gathered in Philadelphia in the sweltering summer of 1787, their task was to revise the Articles of Confederation, the document that loosely bound the colonies together. Instead, they composed a new and radical document, the Constitution, which was printed on September 19th. Whether in broadsides, newspapers, or official government publications, all early printings

Chromolithograph of the
Grand Canyon by Thomas
Moran, 1913

The cornerstone of American exploration: exceedingly rare first edition of the Lewis & Clark Expedition, 1814

of the Constitution are extremely valuable and an essential element of any Americana collection.

That the several states would ratify the new Constitution was not a foregone conclusion. Bitter disagreements over the document divided the framers. *The Federalist*, the famous series of essays in which James Madison, Alexander Hamilton and John Jay advocated ratification, remains a seminal work of political theory. The 1788 first

"Great joy in camp. We are in view of the Ocean, this great Pacific Ocean which we have been so long anxious to see. And the roaring... made by the waves breaking on the rocky shores may be heard distinctly." —William Clark, Journal Entry, November 7, 1805

edition is an obvious cornerstone, but early editions are also desirable, particularly those published within the authors' lifetimes.

Westward expansion continues to fascinate collectors. From the first newspaper accounts of their adventures, Meriwether Lewis and William Clark captured the American imagination. Their definitive account—*History of the Expedition* (1814)—provided a vivid description of the marvels west of the Mississippi and their great map gave the most accurate depiction of the Rocky Mountain regions that the world had yet seen.

To appreciate the progress of America's westward growth, collectors seek out narratives from numerous important nautical and overland voyages. Some of the many significant texts include George Vancouver's *Voyage of Discovery to the North Pacific Ocean* (1798), Alexander Mackenzie's *Voyages from Montreal on the River St. Laurence* (1801), Zebulon Pike's *Account of Expeditions to the Sources of the Mississippi* (1810), and J.C. Fremont's *Report of the Exploring Expedition to the Rocky Mountains* (1845).

Detail from the landmark map published in Lewis and Clark's official account of their expedition, 1814

While others mapped the continent's geography, John James Audubon documented its birds and animals. His monumental illustrated works—*The Birds of America* (first published in four elephant folio volumes, 1827-38) and *The Viviparous Quadrupeds of North America* (three double-elephant folio volumes, 1845-48)—not only expanded ornithological and zoological knowledge but also set a new standard for all naturalist art to come. Audubon's documentary achievement is echoed in three great Native American color plate books of the nineteenth century. George Catlin's dramatically illustrated *North American Indian Portfolio* emerged out of its author's eight years of travel in the Great Plains and Rocky Mountains. Thomas McKenney and James Hall's *History of the Indian Tribes of North America* is not only an ethnographic classic but also one of the great American color plate books, issued in both a splendid large-folio edition and a handsome royal octavo edition. And the vivid, spectacular plates of Karl Bodmer's *Reise in das Innere Nord-America* offer perhaps the most accurate portrayal of Indians as they lived in the Great Plains of the early 1830s.

Original hand-colored portrait of Mehkskeme-Sukahs, Blackfoot Chief, by Karl Bodmer, circa 1843

The first public printing of the Constitution in the *Pennsylvania Packet,* September 19, 1787

The Pennsylvania Packet, and Daily Advertiser.

[Price Four-Pence.]   WEDNESDAY, September 19, 1787.   [No. 2690.]

WE, the People of the United States, in order to form a more perfect Union, establish Justice, insure domestic Tranquility, provide for the common Defence, promote the General Welfare, and secure the Blessings of Liberty to Ourselves and our Posterity, do ordain and establish this Constitution for the United States of America.

ARTICLE I.

Sect. 1. ALL legislative powers herein granted shall be vested in a Congress of the United States, which shall consist of a Senate and House of Representatives.

Sect. 2. The House of Representatives shall be composed of members chosen every second year by the people of the several states, and the electors in each state shall have the qualifications requisite for electors of the most numerous branch of the state legislature.

No person shall be a representative who shall not have attained to the age of twenty-five years, and been seven years a citizen of the United States, and who shall not, when elected, be an inhabitant of that state in which he shall be chosen.

Representatives and direct taxes shall be apportioned among the several states which may be included within this Union, according to their respective numbers, which shall be determined by adding to the whole number of free persons, including those bound to service for a term of years, and excluding Indians not taxed, three-fifths of all other persons. The actual enumeration shall be made within three years after the first meeting of the Congress of the United States, and within every subsequent term of ten years, in such manner as they shall by law direct. The number of representatives shall not exceed one for every thirty thousand, but each state shall have at least one representative; and until such enumeration shall be made, the state of New-Hampshire shall be entitled to chuse three, Massachusetts eight, Rhode-Island and Providence Plantations one, Connecticut five, New-York six, New-Jersey four, Pennsylvania eight, Delaware one, Maryland six, Virginia ten, North-Carolina five, South-Carolina five, and Georgia three.

When vacancies happen in the representation from any state, the Executive authority thereof shall issue writs of election to fill such vacancies.

The House of Representatives shall chuse their Speaker and other officers; and shall have the sole power of impeachment.

Sect. 3. The Senate of the United States shall be composed of two senators from each state chosen by the legislature thereof, for six years; and each senator shall have one vote.

Immediately after they shall be assembled in consequence of the first election, they shall be divided as equally as may be into three classes. The seats of the senators of the first class shall be vacated at the expiration of the second year, of the second class at the expiration of the fourth year, and of the third class at the expiration of the sixth year, so that one-third may be chosen every second year; and if vacancies happen by resignation, or otherwise, during the recess of the Legislature of any state, the Executive thereof may make temporary appointments until the next meeting of the Legislature, which shall then fill such vacancies.

No person shall be a senator who shall not have attained to the age of thirty years, and been nine years a citizen of the United States, and who shall not, when elected, be an inhabitant of that state for which he shall be chosen.

The Vice-President of the United States shall be President of the senate, but shall have no vote, unless they be equally divided.

The Senate shall chuse their other officers, and also a President pro tempore, in the absence of the Vice-President, or when he shall exercise the office of President of the United States.

The Senate shall have the sole power to try all impeachments. When sitting for that purpose, they shall be on oath or affirmation. When the President of the United States is tried, the Chief Justice shall preside: And no person shall be convicted without the concurrence of two-thirds of the members present.

Judgment in cases of impeachment shall not extend further than to removal from office, and disqualification to hold and enjoy any office of honor, trust or profit under the United States; but the party convicted shall nevertheless be liable and subject to indictment, trial, judgment and punishment, according to law.

Sect. 4. The times, places and manner of holding elections for senators and representatives, shall be prescribed in each state by the legislature thereof; but the Congress may at any time by law make or alter such regulations, except as to the places of chusing Senators.

The Congress shall assemble at least once in every year, and such meeting shall be on the first Monday in December, unless they shall by law appoint a different day.

Sect. 5. Each house shall be the judge of the elections, returns and qualifications of its own members, and a majority of each shall constitute a quorum to do business; but a smaller number may adjourn from day to day, and may be authorised to compel the attendance of absent members, in such manner, and under such penalties as each house may provide.

Each house may determine the rules of its proceedings, punish its members for disorderly behaviour, and, with the concurrence of two-thirds, expel a member.

Each house shall keep a journal of its proceedings, and from time to time publish the same, excepting such parts as may in their judgment require secrecy; and the yeas and nays of the members of either house on any question shall, at the desire of one-fifth of those present, be entered on the journal.

Neither house, during the session of Congress, shall, without the consent of the other, adjourn for more than three days, nor to any other place than that in which the two houses shall be sitting.

Sect. 6. The senators and representatives shall receive a compensation for their services, to be ascertained by law, and paid out of the treasury of the United States. They shall in all cases, except treason, felony and breach of the peace, be privileged from arrest during their attendance at

Hand-colored plate of a buffalo from Catlin's *North American Indian Portfolio,* 1844

The Civil War is one of the defining events in American history and collectors seek to understand those crucial years through contemporary and eyewitness accounts. Powerful perspectives are also found in the memoirs of military and political leaders, as well as in comprehensive histories like Francis Trevelyan Miller's *Photographic History of the Civil War,* which contains over a thousand Matthew Brady photographs. Indispensable for any Civil War collection is the *Personal Memoirs* of Ulysses S. Grant, widely regarded as the finest military memoir ever written. Grant, dying of throat cancer, agreed to publish his recollections in order to provide a measure of financial security for his family, and finished the work shortly before his death in the summer of 1885. Mark Twain, who served as publisher, was in awe of the great general's perseverance.

"A book is like a man—clever and dull, brave and cowardly, beautiful and ugly. For every flowering thought there will be a page like a wet and mangy mongrel, and for every looping flight a tap on the wing and a reminder that wax cannot hold the feathers firm too near the sun." — *John Steinbeck*

The one name above all synonymous with the era is that of Lincoln. His texts and speeches reflect the eloquence, intellect and willpower that ultimately secured the future of the Union. His debates with Stephen Douglas, chiefly about the expansion of slavery, were compiled by Lincoln in his earliest important published work. Other landmark Lincoln texts include both of his inaugural addresses, the revered Gettysburg Address and the Emancipation Proclamation. Handsome sets of his writings are desirable, as are insightful and important biographies. And Lincoln autograph material—letters, notes, official certificates, signed government documents—has always been highly valued.

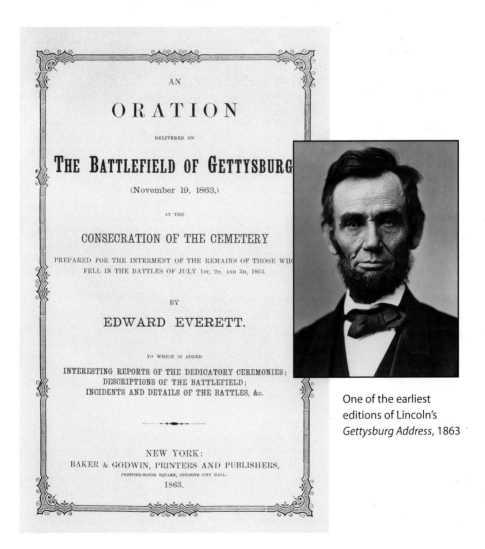

One of the earliest editions of Lincoln's *Gettysburg Address,* 1863

"*Build yourself a book-nest to forget the world without.*"
Abraham Cowley

LITERATURE

O n a winter's day in 1853, one of the most disastrous blazes in the history of
New York City lit up the darkness of Pearl Street. Among other casualties,
the fire claimed the publishing headquarters of Harper & Brothers. Accidentally
ignited, the catastrophic blaze destroyed thousands of books, sheets, plates, and
proofs. Among the many volumes destroyed in the fire were 297 copies of a little-
known book about the obsessive pursuit of an enigmatic white whale. That book
was of course Melville's *Moby-Dick*.

The fire destroyed all but 60 of the remaining unsold copies of this initially
unpopular novel. The publishers had been unenthusiastic in their small printing of
the first American edition and the fire marked the beginning of Melville's descent
into literary oblivion. It was not until the 1920s that interest began to revive in the
work that today has risen from the ashes, casting its stark shadow back over the past
century and transforming the imaginative landscape of the new one.

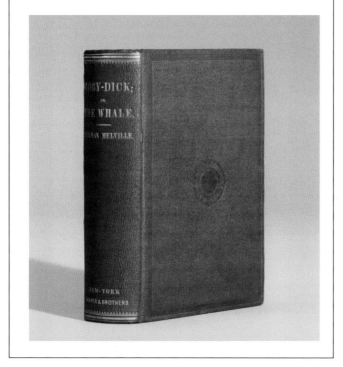

First American
edition of Melville's
Moby-Dick, 1851

"We tell ourselves stories in order to live," wrote Joan Didion. It might also be said that we read great literature in order to remember. Works that add substance to memory, that step into our world so that we live with renewed meaning, continue only as long as these books remain on the shelf. For the collector of rare books, however, it is important not only that the works be read and remembered, but that we pay tribute to each title's earliest or most significant encounters with the world. The rare book collector is inspired by a first edition's profound authority, the resonance of a book lost for decades and newly discovered, the copy with the author's bold signature across a title page or scribbled notes in the margins. These are the rare copies that show us how action and imagination become one force.

For many collectors, a library of ancient classics is a source of inspiration. Though first printings of a work by Homer, Horace or Aristotle are virtually unobtainable, there are fine early translations—from the sixteenth century on—that are accessible to the collector. One may decide to trace the influence of works such as Homer's *Iliad* and *Odyssey* across centuries from the earliest obtainable editions onward, building a collection that might include Chapman's landmark seventeenth century translation (immortalized by Keats' "On first looking into Chapman's Homer") as

Caxton woodcut illustration from "The Knight's Tale"
in Stowe's 1561 edition of Chaucer's *Works*

1676 quarto edition of Shakespeare's *Hamlet,* one of the earliest obtainable separate editions

well as Alexander Pope's celebrated eighteenth century version, a set often found in magnificent period bindings and sometimes containing an original subscriber's notice signed by Pope himself.

Among the greatest of the early English classics are, of course, Chaucer's *Canterbury Tales,* Spenser's *Faerie Queene* and the plays of Shakespeare, which appeared earliest in quarto format and in the four monumental seventeenth-century folio collections. To that list one would add Milton's *Paradise Lost,* Donne's *Poems,* Johnson's *Dictionary* and its companion piece, Boswell's faithfully accurate *Life of Johnson.* Many English classics are acquirable in the first edition. Some of the more elusive include Swift's *Gulliver's Travels,* Defoe's *Robinson Crusoe,* Mary Shelley's *Frankenstein,* and Jane Austen's *Pride and Prejudice.* One of the rarest of all is Emily Brontë's *Wuthering Heights*—thought to have been first printed in an edition as small as 350 copies.

> *"I bequeath myself to the dirt to grow from the grass I love, If you want me again look for me under your boot-soles."*
>
> — *Walt Whitman (his epitaph)*

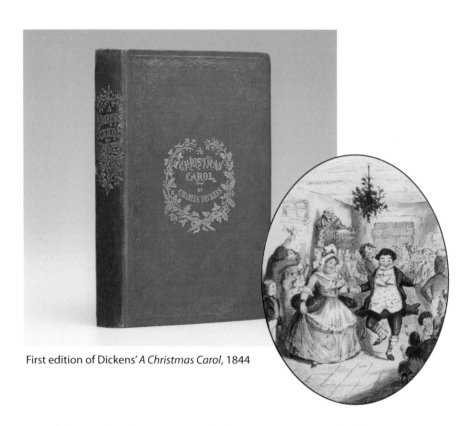

First edition of Dickens' *A Christmas Carol*, 1844

Many of the works of the great English Romantic poets—Shelley, Wordsworth, Byron, Coleridge—are still obtainable in the first editions, as are the works of John Keats. Keats published only three works in his lifetime, and the third, *Lamia,* contains all of his greatest poems, many written during an inspired three-month period before the onset of his final illness. Keats never achieved fame in his lifetime, and thought himself a failure, writing shortly before his death that "I have left no immortal work behind me—nothing to make my friends proud of my memory." Despite his remorse, he is now considered one of the greatest of the English poets, and his small, slim volume, *Lamia,* one of the greatest collections of poems.

Of the myriad great English novelists and playwrights one would want to add to his or her collection—Brontë, Stevenson, Austen, Wells, George Eliot, Fielding, and Wilde, to name a few—Charles Dickens looms large, even today. One of the more prolific writers of his time, Dickens produced a vast body of books that remain modern classics, including *A Tale of Two Cities, Oliver Twist,* and his great autobiographical *David Copperfield.* Dickens' works were issued in various formats; in parts (magazine publications issued monthly), original cloth, and in contemporary bindings. His immortal *Christmas Carol,* amazingly written over a period of just six weeks, is perhaps the most successful of his works and certainly the most influential, as it continues to be an iconic holiday classic.

Turning to America, it is in the nineteenth century that the first great literary and poetical works appear. The essentials for any collection? Cooper's *Last of the Mohicans,* first published in 1826, was the most famous of his Leatherstocking Tales and forever glorified the early American frontier. The incomparable Poe published two remarkable collections of tales between 1840 and 1845; his second collection, entitled simply *Tales,* is considered one of the greatest collections of detective stories ever written, containing such classics as "The Murders in the Rue Morgue." In 1850, after years of modest success, Hawthorne published his finest work, *The Scarlet Letter,* America's first symbolic novel and his greatest success—the first edition reportedly sold out in ten days. The writings of Ralph Waldo Emerson and his friend, Henry David Thoreau, defined the American transcendental movement. Among the latter's works, *Walden* is essential, as is *A Yankee in Canada,* which contained the first publication of his influential essay "Civil Disobedience."

Heading anyone's list is Melville's epic *Moby-Dick,* which first appeared in England under the title *The Whale.* It is among the most difficult of the American firsts to find today, and copies in the original rough cloth binding in fine condition are the most elusive. At its side is Walt Whitman's magnificent *Leaves of Grass.* Whitman published the first edition out of his own meager funds, reportedly assisting with the typesetting himself and overseeing all aspects of the book's production, including its distinctive gilt-stamped green binding. Copies in the original, fragile cloth binding in good condition are extremely scarce and desirable.

It can easily be argued that Mark Twain is the most American of American novelists. It was his achievement to create a literary tradition identified by its respect for the way Americans spoke, in rhythms unique to their region and history, and by its impatience with pretension and hypocrisy. First editions of his best-known novels, the darkly brilliant *Huckleberry Finn* and *Tom Sawyer,* are the centerpieces of any American collection. Also central to any discussion of American traditions is the work of Emily

LITERATURE

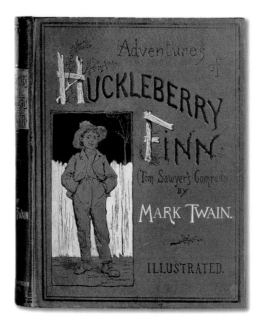

First edition of Mark Twain's *Huckleberry Finn*, 1885

Dickinson. Dickinson, who lived the quietest of lives, published only eleven poems in her lifetime; the three volumes, or series, that first introduced her poetry to the world after her death are exceptionally desirable.

Moving into the modern period, as the world responded to the restless pace of the twentieth century, literature reacted in kind with the realism of classic novels by Crane, Hemingway, and Dreiser and modernism found its champions in the works by key innovators such as Virginia Woolf, T.S. Eliot, and James Joyce. Works by these writers and others of the new century gave birth to a field of rare book collecting defined by the phrase *modern firsts*.

The collector with an eye for the literature of the twentieth century has much to consider, but there are several important points to keep in mind. One is the presence of the dust jacket. A fairly recent innovation to book publishing, the presence and condition of a dust jacket plays a highly significant role in establishing a book's value. It is

> *"The Committee of the Public Library of Concord, Massachusetts, have given us a rattling tip-off puff which will go into every paper in the country. They have expelled Huck from their library as 'trash suitable only for the slums.' That will sell 25,000 copies for us sure."* — Mark Twain

LITERATURE

also important to distinguish first editions from later printings (both of the book and dust jacket), to pay particular attention to any points associated with a first edition, and to be alert to the assets of a valuable inscription or signature. Books signed or inscribed by the author are considerably more valuable than unsigned copies of the same edition, and those that have a notable association or provenance are of particular interest.

During and shortly after World War I, a handful of authors produced a dozen novels and books of poetry that forever changed the path of literature. These cornerstones of modernism, often rejected by the general reading public and widely denounced, sometimes even banned, are among the high spots for collectors of modern firsts. Foremost among these writers is James Joyce. His first work of fiction, *Dubliners,* was the first of a number of his books that he found nearly impossible to get published. He followed with the largely autobiographical *Portrait of the Artist as a Young Man,* which was refused by a total of twelve English printers. It was *Ulysses* that "established Joyce's reputation as perhaps the greatest writer of English prose in the twentieth century—perhaps in any century" (Parker). Banned on both sides of the Atlantic, the first edition was printed in Paris in an edition of 1000 copies. Bound in distinctive and

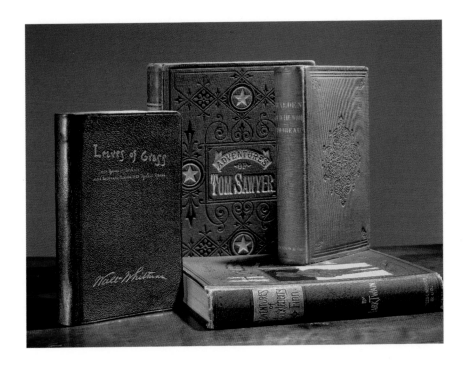

LITERATURE

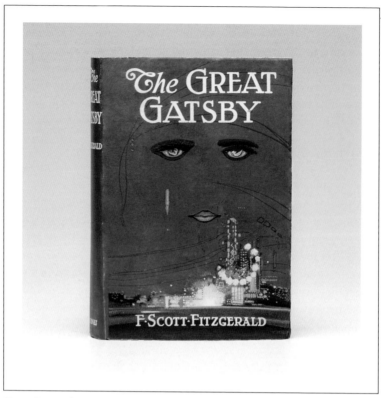

First edition of *The Great Gatsby*, in the extraordinarily rare original dust jacket

fragile blue paper wrappers, *Ulysses* is highly sought after by collectors and certainly stands as the centerpiece of any modern literature collection.

The 1920s saw an explosion of great writers and books. Ernest Hemingway's *In Our Time*, *The Sun Also Rises*, and *A Farewell to Arms*, F. Scott Fitzgerald's *The Great Gatsby*, T.S. Eliot's *The Waste Land*, William Faulkner's *The Sound and the Fury*, Virginia Woolf's *A Room of One's Own*, D.H. Lawrence's *Lady Chatterley's Lover*: all were first published in that remarkable decade. All are acquirable for the collector, though some are more elusive than others. *The Great Gatsby*, *The Sun Also Rises* and *The Sound and the Fury* have the distinction of being three of the most sought-after modern firsts in the original dust jackets.

> *"So we beat on, boats against the current, borne back ceaselessly into the past."* —F. Scott Fitzgerald, *The Great Gatsby*

The list of modern firsts that would qualify for any great collection is extensive. Included would be J. D. Salinger's controversial masterpiece *The Catcher in the Rye*, William Golding's allegorical *Lord of the Flies*, Harper Lee's great American classic *To Kill a Mockingbird*, George Orwell's cautionary tales *Animal Farm* and *1984*, John Steinbeck's epic of the Great Depression *The Grapes of Wrath*, Ayn Rand's influential *Atlas Shrugged*, Joseph Heller's scathing indictment of war *Catch-22*, Ken Kesey's equally scathing indictment of the American mental institutions *One Flew Over the Cuckoo's Nest*, and Jack Kerouac's rambling, brilliant American journey *On the Road*.

This is, of course, only a sampling of the works of literature that one could place in the canon of the great and collectible. Author and critic Italo Calvino wrote, "A classic is a book that has never finished saying what it has to say." As overwhelmed as we might be considering the range and sheer number of important works of literature produced through the centuries, one of the fascinations of collecting is that by seeking out the books we think are most important, we bring a certain order to the great expanse and preserve in our collections those books that had a significance for us—as individuals and as a society.

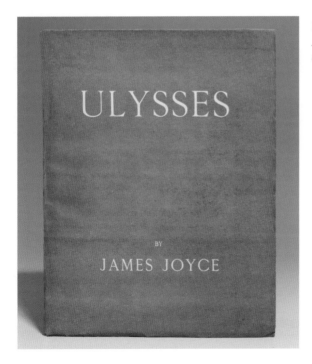

First edition of James Joyce's *Ulysses* in the original paper wrappers

LITERATURE

"*Without the word, without the writing of books, there is no history, there is no concept of humanity.*" *Herman Hesse*

TRAVEL AND EXPLORATION

In 1772 Captain James Cook, determined to either find or disprove the existence of *Terra Australis*, set sail on the *HMS Resolution*. This was his second of three voyages to the Pacific; on his first voyage Cook and his men were the first recorded Europeans to view Australia's eastern coastline. On his second voyage he conclusively disproved the existence of the fabled southern continent and became one of the first to cross the Antarctic Circle. Each of Cook's three voyages was soon followed by a published account detailing the expedition's routes, discoveries and contacts with native peoples, flora and fauna. Each chronicle was richly illustrated with

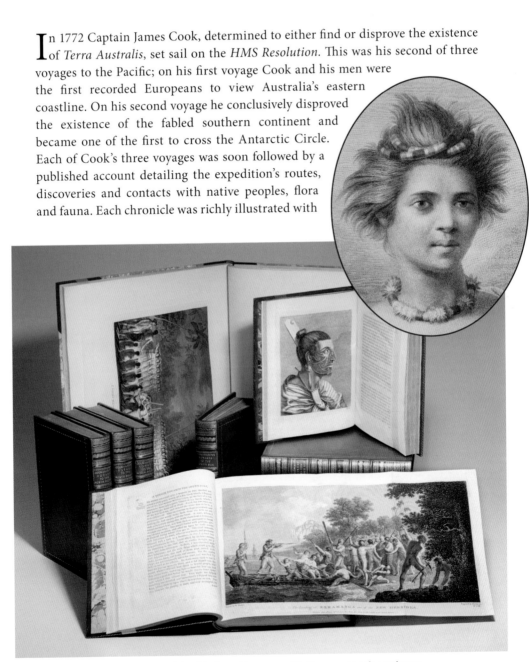

Complete first edition set of Cook's three *Voyages*, with the scarce atlas volume

engravings; the report of Cook's tragically fatal third voyage was accompanied by an elephant folio atlas volume containing more than 60 large, detailed engravings.

A number of Cook's junior officers continued the exploration of the Pacific after Cook's untimely death. The most famous of these is undoubtedly William Bligh, Cook's former sailing master, who was given command of the *HMS Bounty* and charged with sailing to Tahiti to collect breadfruit. In 1789, Master's Mate Fletcher Christian led his famed bloodless mutiny, setting Bligh and 18 loyal crewmen adrift in the ship's launch. In "one of the most heroic sea voyages ever made," with nothing more than a sextant and a pocket watch, Bligh navigated this small open boat in an epic 41-day journey across 3600 nautical miles to Timor. In 1790, he published his gripping account, *The Narrative of the Mutiny on Board HMS Bounty*.

> *"Ambition leads me not only farther than any other man has been before me, but as far as I think it possible for man to go." — The Journal of Captain James Cook*

Of the non-English expeditions sent to challenge English supremacy in the vast Pacific, the most notable is the French expedition of 1785-88 commanded by La Pérouse, whose richly illustrated *Voyage autour du Monde* was first published posthumously in French in 1797 and in English in 1799. His and other early Pacific voyages opened the routes to trade with Japan, China and other Asian nations, leading the way to historic diplomatic missions such as Commodore Matthew Perry's visit to the region in 1852-54, recounted and vividly illustrated in his *Narrative of the Expedition to the China Seas and Japan* (1856).

Henry Stanley

TRAVEL AND
EXPLORATION

Illustration from Matthew Perry's *Expedition to Japan*, 1856

Africa is another major area of interest for collectors of travel literature. Of the many books chronicling the exploration of Africa, perhaps the most famous is New York journalist Henry Stanley's dramatic account of his search for the lost missionary and explorer David Livingstone.

Many collectors also focus on the history of a single figure, such as the brilliant nineteenth-century explorer Richard Burton. Most famous for being one of the first Europeans to undertake the *hajj* to Mecca in the guise of a Muslim—detailed in his justly renowned and highly sought-after *Personal Narrative of a Pilgrimage to El-Medinah and Mecca*—this intrepid adventurer also traveled extensively in Africa, India, the western United States and South America. T.E. Lawrence—Lawrence of Arabia—is an equally enigmatic and compelling figure, whose classic narrative of his service in the Arab Revolt during World War I, *The Seven Pillars of Wisdom* (1926), was deemed by Winston Churchill "one of the greatest books in the English language."

TRAVEL AND EXPLORATION

> *"No person who has not spent a period of his life in those 'stark and sullen solitudes that sentinel the Pole' will understand fully what trees and flowers, sun-flecked turf and running streams mean to the soul of a man."* —Ernest Shackleton

The dramatic races to both the North and South Poles consumed the lives of men, the resources of nations and the attention of millions. Robert Scott and Ernest Shackleton each assembled worthy teams and made valiant attempts to reach the South Pole, recorded in *The Voyage of the 'Discovery'* (1905) and *The Heart of the Antarctic* (1909). Norwegian Roald Amundsen succeeded where the Englishmen failed, in part because he used dogs rather than men to pull equipment and because his men wore fur clothing rather than the wool used by the British teams. He reached the Pole 34 days ahead of Scott, as chronicled in his richly illustrated two-volume work *The South Pole* (1913).

Illustrations from the deluxe signed limited edition of Shackleton's *Heart of the Antarctic*

TRAVEL AND EXPLORATION

Lithograph of the Sphinx from Roberts' *Holy Land*

The inclusion of hand-colored lithographs, maps, woodcuts, photographs or engraved plates found in many of the classic works of exploration and travel make this field of collecting a rich visual experience. Few can resist the splendidly illustrated travel books of the late eighteenth and early nineteenth centuries.

Coinciding with the expansion of the British Empire, English travel books met a public demand for faithful and fine images of the foreign lands that were so crucially important to the Empire. At the turn of the nineteenth century, Thomas and William Daniell produced several books of beautiful hand-colored aquatint illustrations of life and monuments in India and China that were immediately popular and are still avidly sought-after by collectors. Many feel that lithography reached its zenith in David Roberts' magnificent folio work *The Holy Land* (1846-49), an extensive collection of 250 tinted lithographs finely colored by hand. Mixing the romantic with the realistic, Roberts' depictions of the renowned sites of Jerusalem, Egypt, Syria and Arabia are highlights of illustrated travel literature.

**TRAVEL AND
EXPLORATION**

"Some books are undeservedly forgotten;
none are undeservedly remembered." W. H. Auden

CHILDREN'S CLASSICS

Once upon a time, children's books weren't necessarily—or even usually—fun. It sounds strange today, when toddlers *Pat the Bunny*, beginning readers sound out a menu of *Green Eggs and Ham* and throngs attend midnight bookstore parties for the release of Harry Potter's latest adventure. But education, not entertainment, drove the earliest literature for young readers. Engraved emblem books presented children with stern morality tales, horn books introduced them to their ABCs and 123s, and the New England Primer imparted to them the essential tenets of Calvinist doctrine.

Of course, children still recognized and adored good stories when they found them. Why should grown-ups get all the fun from Aesop's fables, fairy tales by Charles Perrault, Hans Christian Andersen, and the Brothers Grimm and the *Arabian Nights*? Granted, some stories originally aimed at adults—the allegorical *Pilgrim's Progress* of Bunyan, the satirical *Gulliver's Travels* by Swift, the adventurous *Robinson Crusoe* by Defoe—were often abridged and adapted for a younger audience. Even so, morality and manners remained the mainstay of children's literature.

Illustration from Lewis Carroll's *Alice in Wonderland*

First edition of
Peter Rabbit, 1902

But then in 1865, a little girl named Alice fell down a rabbit-hole, taking countless devoted readers with her. Through nonsense and nimble wordplay, aided and abetted by John Tenniel's enchanting drawings, Lewis Carroll liberated children's literature from sentimental shackles and religious restraints in *Alice's Adventures in Wonderland* (1865) and its sequel, *Through the Looking-Glass* (1871)—the latter book, incidentally, was a phenomenon of its day, garnering some 15,500 pre-publication orders. Carroll's relentlessly logical lunacy demolished people's expectations of what children's books were and set new standards for what they could be.

The twentieth century saw the birth of more cherished children's characters. In an illustrated letter to a friend's ill child, Beatrix Potter first told *The Tale of Peter Rabbit*; unable to find a publisher, Potter produced the first edition in 1901 herself in a run of only 250 copies. J.M. Barrie made audiences believe in fairies and a boy who wouldn't grow up, first on

"My own favorite amongst my little books": Illustration from Potter's *Tailor of Gloucester*

stage (1904) and later on the page in his Peter Pan tale. And, in four books first published from 1924 to 1928, A.A. Milne spun stories and poems about his son, Christopher Robin, and the child's favorite toys—most especially one ever-clumsy, always-hungry Edward Bear, better known as "Pooh." The subtle and intuitive line drawings of Ernest H. Shepard (whose daughter, Mary, would also illustrate children's books—she provided the pictures of P.L. Travers' "practically perfect" *Mary Poppins*) are as integral a part of the "Pooh Quartet" as are Milne's lyrical, witty and often insightful texts.

Shepard was one of the last prominent illustrators of the "Golden Age" of children's literature. Many before him had helped enchant readers, young and old. The brothers Grimm admired George Cruikshank's illustrations for their *German Popular Stories* (1823-26) so much that they virtually elevated his Gothic-style pictures to "official" status, insisting on their presence in future editions. Walter Crane, a pioneer in color picture books, relished the chance to illustrate children's literature because he believed it was "perhaps the only outlet for unrestrained flights of fancy open to the modern illustrator, who likes to revolt against the despotism of facts." Delicate, charming children grace the pages of Kate Greenaway's books, while more boisterous subjects romp their way through Randolph Caldecott's art.

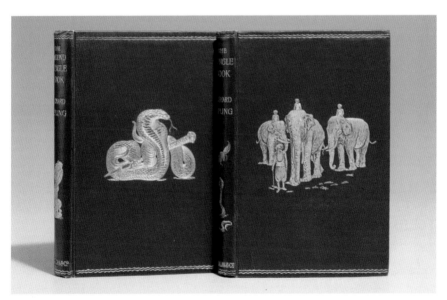

First editions of Kipling's *Jungle Books*, in original cloth-gilt bindings

First edition of Baum's
The Wonderful Wizard of Oz

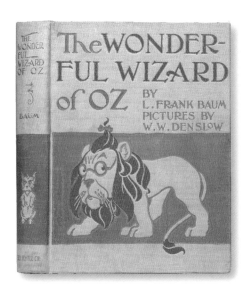

In America, Howard Pyle led the way for book illustrators with such volumes as *The Merry Adventures of Robin Hood*, *The Wonder Clock*, and four volumes of Arthurian legend. Pyle not only illustrated but also wrote these books; in addition, he taught and inspired the next generation of great American book illustrators. Pyle's students included N.C. Wyeth, who made his name with his illustrations for Scribner's 1911 edition of *Treasure Island*; Maxfield Parrish, whose vibrant illustrations for Louise Saunders' play *The Knave of Hearts* perfectly capture the whimsy of nursery rhymes; and Jessie Willcox Smith, who is renowned especially for her beautiful 1916 illustrations for Charles Kingsley's *The Water Babies*.

The two artists still contending with each other in critics' debates for the title of the greatest illustrator of "Golden Age" children's literature are Arthur Rackham—noted for such sumptuous gift books as *Rip Van Winkle* (1905), *Peter Pan in Kensington Gardens* (1906) and *Alice in Wonderland* (1907)—and Edmund Dulac. His innovative use of color and creative appropriation of Near Eastern elements yielded some of the most striking images children's books had yet seen: the sleepless princess atop her mountain of mattresses, the heartbreakingly beautiful Snow Queen enthroned regally in frozen solitude, and the Emperor admiring his nightingale by a lantern's soft glow.

American authors helped populate the pantheon of children's books. L. Frank Baum led the way in 1900 with *The Wonderful Wizard of Oz*, his attempt to tell an American-style fairy tale "in which the wonderment and joy are retained and the heart-aches and nightmares are left out."

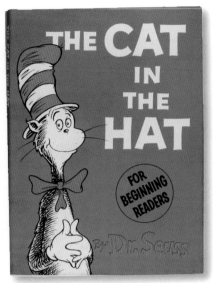

First edition of Dr. Seuss'
Cat in the Hat

Baum's bright and boisterous fairyland proved so popular that he wrote thirteen sequels. Other authors continued the series after his death in 1919, but that magical first book, with its seamless integration of Baum's text and W.W. Denslow's brilliantly colorful illustrations, remains the artistic landmark against which all other modern fairy tales are measured.

An equally magical breakthrough by another American author occurred in 1957. Theodor Geisel, using a vocabulary of just over 200 words, described the visit of *The Cat in the Hat* to two bored children (and their nervous fish) on a rainy Saturday afternoon. The Cat's antics, breezily related at an aggressive pace, enthralled youngsters, much as the nonsense of Lewis Carroll had entranced his readers some 90 years earlier. Just as important, Seuss' skillful use of repetition, rhythm and rhyme helped young readers build their skills—an educational aim true to the origins of literature for children. All of Seuss' children's books instruct and entertain, encouraging all who read them, young or not so young, to expand their imaginations and experience new possibilities.

The same can be said of all great children's books. Edward Lear's limericks and Shel Silverstein's silly songs... the eerily elegant fairy creatures of Kay Nielsen, the persevering insects of Eric Carle and the rumpusing Wild Things of Maurice Sendak... the court at Camelot, the asteroid of the Little Prince and, yes, even Hogwarts: the best children's literature inspires us all.

On Collecting
CHILDREN'S BOOKS

"Freedom of thought is best promoted by the gradual illumination of men's minds, which follows from the advance of science..." Charles Darwin

SCIENCE AND NATURAL HISTORY

William Hazlitt defined science as "the desire to know causes," and the collector of rare scientific and natural history books shares that passion. The great works of mathematics, chemistry, physics, biology, botany and astronomy represent not only the investigation of the hidden causes that move the visible world, but also the celebration of the human curiosity, research and insight that made such investigation possible, and those revolutionary shifts in human thought that made the mysterious understandable.

Often collectors of science begin with the early editions or translations of works by Ptolemy, Euclid, and Archimedes, or with first editions of landmark books by Galileo, Copernicus and Newton. The collector may focus on one branch of science, following the advances of research in a particular field, or trace the work of a single scientist from the earliest papers published in journals through published books, correspondence and biographies. Marie Curie, Charles Darwin, and Albert Einstein

**SCIENCE &
NATURAL HISTORY**

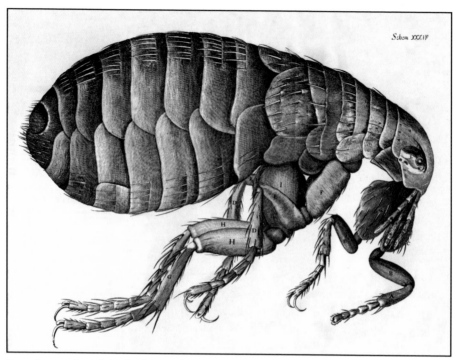
Famed engraving of the flea from Robert Hooke's *Micrographia*, 1665

are a few of the figures who inspire collections built around their remarkable contributions. Collections might be formed of the works of Nobel Prize-winners, for example, or trace the progress of technology from the steam engine to the computer.

What are some landmark books that one might find in a great science collection? Perhaps a first edition of Galileo's *Dialogo*, his famous defense of the Copernican system which led to his persecution by the Inquisition. First published in 1632, it was formally condemned by the church in 1633 and remained on the index of prohibited books for nearly two centuries. Another landmark is Newton's *Principia Mathematica*, considered one of the most important books in the history of science. The first edition, published in Latin in 1687, is extraordinarily rare, as few as 300 copies were printed, only half of which are thought to be extant. The first English edition, which is also quite uncommon, made its appearance in 1729. Robert Hooke's *Micrographia* gave the public its first glimpse at a hitherto unseen world in 1665 through his recently developed compound microscope. Moving across centuries, a high spot for any collection would be the original offprint of Watson and Crick's article announcing the structure of DNA.

Darwin's *On the Origin of Species*, where science and natural history intersect, is central. Huxley called it "the most potent instrument for the extension of the realm of natural knowledge," and there is little doubt that the successful first edition—which reportedly sold out in a single day—is one of the most influential books in history. Darwin accomplished his researches during the age of the great plate books, in which the animals, birds and plants from the most exotic regions of the world were being catalogued, documented and illustrated for an eager public. Darwin himself, on his return from the Galapagos Islands, consulted with one of the foremost ornithologists of the day, John Gould, who over a period of some fifty years produced one of the most important and beautiful series of plate books depicting the birds from every region of the globe. When one turns to the catalogue of great natural history books produced in the nineteenth century, the sheer scale and workmanship of these volumes is remarkable. Audubon's great elephant folios of the birds of North America, in which he tried to replicate the figures in their actual sizes, was the result of many years of first-hand observation under the most difficult of circumstances. Today it is one of the rarest and most valuable books in the world.

Hand-colored lithograph from Audubon's monumental *Quadrupeds of North America*

SCIENCE &
NATURAL HISTORY

MEDICINE

For centuries smallpox devastated the world. Those who survived the disease were immune to recurrences, and it was a widely held belief that milkmaids who had contracted cowpox, a relatively benign cousin of smallpox caught from cattle, also developed immunity. Country doctor Edward Jenner decided to make an experiment: on May 14, 1796 he injected cowpox lymph from an infected milkmaid into a country boy, James Phipps. A few weeks later he inoculated Phipps with the smallpox virus. No infection developed, a result which lead to "one of the greatest triumphs in the history of medicine," the eventual eradication of the deadly disease (Garrison & Morton). In the work he published, at his own expense, *An Inquiry into the Causes and Effects of the Variolae Vaccinae* (1798), Jenner described the results of his experiments, using the term "virus" for the first time.

For the collector of great medical works many similar dramatic breakthroughs await. *The Workes of that Famous Chirurgion [Surgeon] Ambrose Parey*, first published in English translation in 1634, describes a number of that military surgeon's field-tested advancements, among them treating gunshot wounds with a revolutionary mix of egg yolks, oil of roses and turpentine instead of the traditional—and much more painful—cauterization with boiling water. In 1819 (translated into English two years later), R.T.H. Laennec, in his *Treatise of the Diseases of the Chest*, detailed how he used a hollow

Hand-colored lithograph from Quain's *Anatomy*, 1836

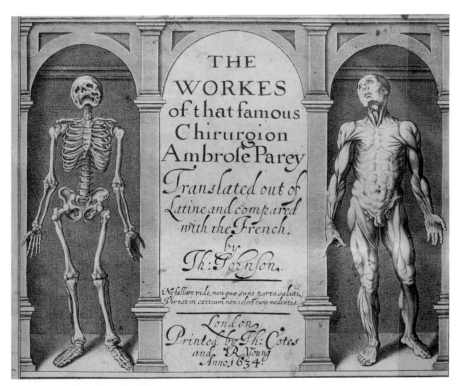

Title page from the 1634 first edition of Parey's *Works*

tube of wood to amplify the beating of his patients' hearts—the invention of the stethoscope, accompanied by an engraved illustration of this new tool. Henry Gray was only 33 years old in 1858 when he published his landmark text, *Anatomy Descriptive and Surgical*, which would become the standard anatomical reference for generations of students and practicing physicians.

Anatomical atlases rank among the most beautiful and finely detailed books ever produced. Tracing a long line of distinguished descent from Johannes de Ketham's *Fasciculus Medicinae* (1495) and Andreas Vesalius' splendid *De Humani Corporis* (1543) through such landmarks as William Cowper's *The Anatomy of Humane Bodies* (1698) and William Cheselden's *Osteographia, or Anatomy of the Bones* (1733)—all monumental folio masterpieces of the art of engraving—the collector of such works follows the development of both the art and the science of medicine through the centuries. Later works such as George Spratt's *Obstetric Tables* (1833)—with plates featuring movable flaps—and Jones Quain's five-volume folio *Series of Anatomical Plates* (1836-42) demonstrate how medical knowledge advanced.

MEDICINE

ARTISTS' BOOKS

Artists' books—also known as *livres d'artiste*—provide the collector with an excellent opportunity to own original works produced specifically for that book and signed by an important artist. At times the marriage of an artist with a classic text is a particularly happy one, as when Salvador Dalí created twelve original lithographs to accompany the surreal dreamscape of *Alice's Adventures in Wonderland*. This beautifully produced large portfolio was issued in 1969 in an edition of 2500 copies; after publication the original lithographic stones used to print the images were destroyed, ensuring that no further editions would be produced—a common practice of the *livre d'artiste*, adding to its appeal for collectors.

Original lithograph from Dalí's *Alice in Wonderland*

We find an equally felicitous combination in the 1934 Limited Editions Club version of Aristophanes' *Lysistrata*, the only American publication with original Picasso etchings, or in the same publisher's 1935 limited edition of James Joyce's masterpiece *Ulysses*, with original illustrations by Matisse. The author and the artist were both supposed to sign 1500 copies together; when it became apparent to Joyce that not only had Matisse not read his novel prior to making his illustrations, but had in fact based his sketches instead on Homer's *Odyssey*, the indignant author stormed out of the signing, leaving only 250 of the proposed 1500 copies signed by both men.

A cousin of the *livre d'artiste* is the illustrated gift book, lavishly produced and particularly popular in the early twentieth century. Arthur Rackham, Edmund Dulac, Maxfield Parrish, N.C. Wyeth, Howard Pyle and other renowned artists were commissioned to illustrate classic texts, including *Peter Pan in Kensington Gardens, The Rubaiyat of Omar Khayyam, The Knave of Hearts, The Yearling,* and *The Story of King Arthur and His Knights,* to name a few. These gift books were often printed on thick handmade paper in quarto format to allow for larger prints of the artists' original paintings, richly rendered in the new three-color process and tipped onto heavy paper. Publishers would typically issue these fine books bound in creamy vellum with pictorial gilt decorations and silk ties.

First illustrated edition of *Ulysses,* one of only 250 copies signed by both Joyce and Matisse

PHOTOGRAPHY

Whether in snapshot, portrait, calotype, positive or negative, panorama, daguerreotype or print, the all-powerful eye of the camera has launched one of the fastest growing fields for the rare book collector to explore. With both art and technology in its genes, photography bridges centuries, tracing its origins back to our earliest speculations about vision, sunlight's transformative mysteries, and the delights of the *camera obscura*. Part magic, part memory, with painting as a forefather and cinema a second cousin, this is a fascinating area.

Glancing at a picture of his mother, taken when she was a child, Roland Barthes described the experience. "I studied the little girl," he wrote, "and at last discovered my mother." It is the photograph's intimacy and this capacity to bring life to history—in all its dimensions—that draws so many to the field. For photographers

such as Edward Weston or Ansel Adams, that impulse produced an incomparable record of America's unique landscape.

For collectors who find humanity's greatest truths in its harshest moments, the war photography of Mathew Brady, Robert Capa, Margaret Bourke-White or James Nachtwey are fundamental starting points. For those who value the history of a people captured in a photograph, the work of Edward Curtis, with its turn-of-the-century portraits of Native Americans, has achieved considerable stature.

The city has inspired photography in countless ways. The works of Eugène Atget, Brassaï, André Kertész, William Klein, Henri Cartier-Bresson, Berenice Abbott, Weegee, or Bruce Davidson, to name but a few, are highly recommended. Rural landscapes and their people

Sepia photogravure of a Nambe girl from Edward Curtis' monumental work on North American Indians

have their own distinctive images and stories, as well, and the brilliance of an image by Walker Evans, Dorothea Lange, Wright Morris, Robert Frank or Doris Ulman tells these tales in unforgettable ways. Suburbia is not to be left behind either; both Lee Friedlander and William Eggleston have their own stirring images to offer.

But the collector need not focus strictly on a place or a time, a culture or even an event. For those interested in tracing photography's link to other arts, the works of Alfred Stieglitz, Man Ray, Paul Strand or Edward Steichen offer a promising introduction to the subject. The fashion photography of Richard Avedon, Bruce Weber or Irving Penn is fascinating for its insight into the business of beauty. Similarly, the rhythmic simplicity of works by Karl Blossfeldt or Bernhard and Hilla Becher sculpt technology into unforgettable signatures of iron and steel.

"History with its flickering lamp stumbles along the trail of the past..."
Winston Churchill

HISTORY

W.H. Auden said, "man is a history-making creature who can neither repeat his past nor leave it behind." For Auden, our impulse to record the past is fundamental—instinctual. Whether your interest leads along academic or highly personal routes, whether you are in search of first-hand accounts or histories narrated by later voices, a collection built around classic histories can be fascinating.

One of the earliest history books is also one of the best, a true cornerstone for any collector: Hartmann Schedel's *Liber Chronicarum*, more popularly known as the Nuremberg Chronicle. First published in 1493 in Latin and German editions, this monumental folio history of the world is one of the greatest illustrated books ever published. It contains the first modern map of Europe, as well as Ptolemy's map of the world, and nearly every page is embellished with woodcuts, some by the young Albrecht Dürer.

You might also consider fine English translations of works by Plutarch, Livy, Pliny, Suetonius, Josephus, Herodotus, Thucydides or Xenophon. The influence of these can be traced through much of Western history. The translations of Raphael Holinshed and Sir Thomas North, or Sir Thomas Malory's *Le Morte D'Arthur,* were stepping stones for generations of writers, philosophers and statesmen. For the collector interested in pursuing this evolution, other major works to consider might be Philemon Holland's translation of Plutarch's *Morals*, with its great impact on the 1612 edition of Bacon's *Essays*, or Holland's translation of Suetonius' dramatic biographies of the Caesars, which for years established the prototype for subsequent biographies.

Walter Raleigh

In any collection of historical works Edward Gibbon's *History of the Decline and Fall of the Roman Empire* must certainly have a place. Almost universally esteemed from the time of its publication, it "has remained one of the ageless historical works" (PMM). Other important works by European historians include David Hume's *History of Great Britain*, Thomas Carlyle's *French Revolution*, Edward Clarendon's *History of the Rebellion and Civil Wars in England*, Raleigh's *The History of the World*, William Camden's history of Elizabeth I, Raphael Holinshed's *Chronicles*, the works of Richard Hooker and accounts of Napoleon's life and career.

The twentieth century was a time of rapid technological and medical advances, two devastating world wars, utopian visionaries and social upheaval. Many collectors seek the works and signatures of those figures who during this time—to paraphrase Shakespeare—were born great, achieved greatness, or had greatness thrust upon them.

In addition to his political accomplishments, Winston Churchill was also one of the finest historians of the century. Among his many writings, Churchill's comprehensive studies of the two world wars, *The World Crisis* (published in six

Hand-colored woodcut illustration from the *Nuremberg Chronicle*, 1493

volumes, 1923-31) and *The Second World War* (also published in six volumes, 1948-53), are two of his most popular titles.

Political accounts penned by those who lead nations and people through turbulent times give us insight into their particular challenges and choices. Perhaps the most popular of John F. Kennedy's several books is his Pulitzer Prize-winning *Profiles in Courage*, a series of sketches of American politicians who risked their careers for their principles. Martin Luther King also wrote a number of influential books, among them *Why We Can't Wait*, which includes his famous "Letter from Birmingham Jail." This book was published in 1964, the year he won the Nobel Peace Prize, and responds directly to the Kennedy assassination. "Foremost among the founding fathers of Israel," political leader and writer David Ben-Gurion drafted the nation's Declaration of Independence and served as the first Prime Minister. First editions signed or inscribed by any of these leaders, while often rare and quite sought-after, bring the collector that much closer to the momentous events their authors lived through—and to their powerful dreams for the future.

"When we build, let us think that we build forever." Frank Lloyd Wright

ARCHITECTURE

In the early eighteenth century Giacomo Leoni's translation into English of Andrea Palladio's *I Quattro libri dell'architettura* (first published in 1570) solidified the late Renaissance architect's reputation and led to the revival of his classical architectural theories, sparking the movement that became known as Palladianism. Thomas Jefferson had many copies of Palladio's *Four Books* in his library and used them as a basis for his design of Monticello. "Palladio is the Bible," he told a friend whom he urged to get a copy of the treatise, "and stick close to it" (Randall, 151). Many other sumptuous architectural and artistic plate books were published in the first half of the eighteenth century, including Colin Campbell's richly illustrated *Vitruvius Britannicus, or the British Architect* (1715-25) in three folio volumes, William Kent's folio *Designs of Inigo Jones* (1727), and William Newton's illustrated English translation of the *Architecture of M. Vitruvius Pollio* (1771-91) in two folio volumes. It is no coincidence that in 1721,

Ackermann's *History of the Abbey Church*

while English architects were seeking inspiration in classical models, Leonardo Da Vinci's *A Treatise of Painting* would make its first appearance in English, illustrated with 35 finely engraved plates. Palladio wasn't the only prominent architect from the Italian Renaissance to have a profound impact on architectural theory and practice in the coming centuries. When Sebastiano Serlio's richly illustrated folio *Five Bookes of Architecture* appeared in English in 1611 (first published in Italian in 1537-47), it represented "one of the earliest English manifestations of the interest in architectural literature spawned by the Renaissance" (Avery). Giacomo Barozzi da Vignola was "another of the great protagonists of the Italian Renaissance, as influential in France as Palladio was in England" (Fowler); his *The Regular Architect* first appeared in English in 1669 (first published in Italian in 1562), illustrated with folio copperplate engravings.

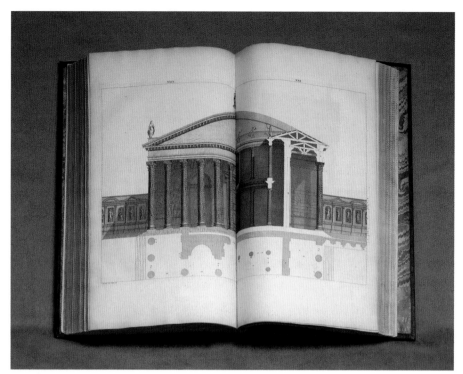

Palladio's *Four Books of Architecture*

In the first half of the next century publisher Rudolph Ackermann made good use of the relatively new aquatint printing technology to meet the public's demand for lavishly illustrated views of famous cathedrals (*History of the Abbey Church*, two volumes, 1812), renowned universities (*History of the University of Oxford*, two volumes, 1814; *History of the University of Cambridge*, two volumes, 1815) and picturesque landscapes (*Picturesque Tour along the Rhine*, 1820; *Picturesque Tour of the English Lakes*, 1821). Ackermann issued all of his works in lovely folio volumes filled with delicately hand-colored aquatint engravings that seemed more like collections of watercolor paintings than printed images. William Henry Pyne, a watercolorist and one-time collaborator with Ackermann, issued his ambitious *History of the Royal Residences* in three folio volumes in 1819 in the grand Ackermann tradition. The expense of producing this sumptuously illustrated work landed Pyne in debtor's prison and kept him from becoming a long-term rival of Ackermann. "The books adorned by colored aquatint engraving remain among the most attractive in the history of illustration" (Ray, 29).

The eighteenth-century tradition of the folio plate book of architectural drawings continues in Frank Lloyd Wright's monumental *Buildings, Plans and Designs* (1963), an impressive portfolio of 100 plates of his earliest designs. Wright's theories of architecture and urban planning can be found in *Modern Architecture* (1931), a compilation of the Kahn Lectures he delivered at Princeton, *The Disappearing City* (1932), in which he proposed a decentralized, agrarian society, and *The Future of Architecture* (1953). The theories, designs, plans and finished works of Wright's heirs—architectural stars such as Frank Gehry, Philip Johnson, Ludwig Mies van der Rohe and Rem Koolhaas—are highly sought after as well.

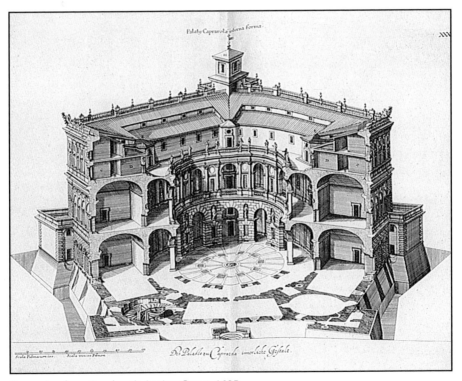

Engraving from Sandrart's *Ancient Rome*, 1685

ARCHITECTURE

"When I am attacked by gloomy thoughts, nothing helps me so much as running to my books." *Michel de Montaigne*

PHILOSOPHY AND LAW

Great ideas in philosophy may represent the spirit of their age, or dissect it, but their influence is seldom limited to one field or discipline. For who could persuasively argue that the works of Plato or Aristotle are not profoundly resonant in medicine, architecture, literature, and music?

First editions of early translations of these philosophers, along with the later figures of the Renaissance and the Reformation, are ready points of departure for any collector with an avid interest in tracing the development of Western thought. Whether a collector's interest focuses on the works of Wittgenstein, Nietzsche or Descartes, on Spinoza's claims for the independence of philosophy and religion, on the moral authority of Pascal, on Hume's attempt to build a theory of knowledge, or on Rousseau's eloquent proposal of a social contract, the informed pursuit of philosophical classics occupies a significant place in the continuance of these ideas.

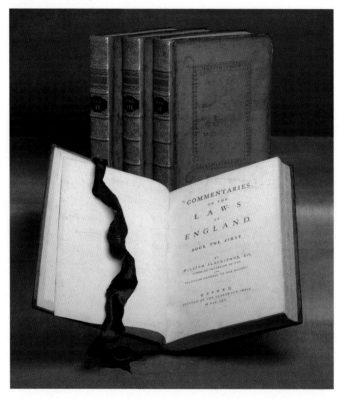

Blackstone's *Commentaries on the Laws of England*, 1765-69

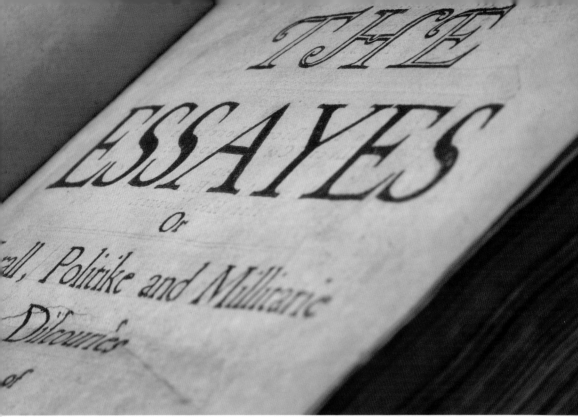

Montaigne's *Essayes*, 1603

Because works of philosophy have historically been widely influential, their effect can be readily glimpsed in the turbulence of the state and its laws. In Locke's *Essay Concerning Human Understanding*, for example, we find the first "attempt to estimate crucially the certainty and the adequacy of human knowledge when confronted with God and the universe" (PMM). His conclusions helped fuel the Enlightenment and ultimately the convictions of America's founding fathers. Similarly, in Hobbes' *Leviathan*, one of the most controversial and important tracts ever written in political philosophy, we find another key influence on the framers of the Constitution.

"During the early years of the Revolutionary period," for example, "American leaders found Locke's revolutionary compact ideas more useful than Hobbes' view of the unlimited authority of the state. But as the political and social experience of the 1780s seemed to bear out Hobbes' pessimistic view that men are essentially self-interested, the Hobbesian outlook became more relevant. When John Adams wrote that 'he who would found a state, and make proper laws for the government of it, must presume that all men are bad by nature,' he was expressing an idea that was derived at once from Hobbes" (*A Covenanted People*).

Because of philosophy's close comradeship to history, a collector might find immense satisfaction in building a library that situates thought in the midst of action. The great works of Nicolo Machiavelli or Edmund Burke, Mary Wollstonecraft or Thomas Paine have an inexhaustible reach.

In classics of the law, as well, the collector might pursue philosophy's practical bent. Hugo Grotius, Oliver Wendell Holmes, Jr., Abraham Lincoln, Edward Coke and William Blackstone are but a sampling of the great legal thinkers whose works might well spark a collector's curiosity and passion. Classic printings of the Magna Carta, or early printings of key documents in U.S. history, among them the Stamp Act, Revolutionary War pamphlets and acts, or works documenting the Supreme Court's later rulings on segregation—any of these would be significant additions to a collector's library.

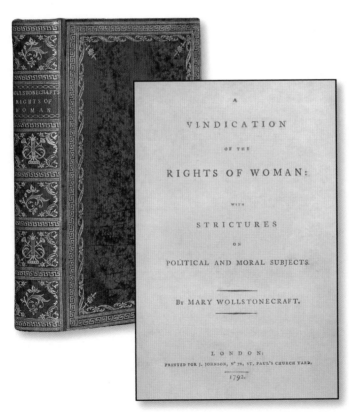

First edition of Mary Wollstonecraft's *Vindication of the Rights of Woman*, 1792

ECONOMICS

Though some might think that work and money, property and trade, banking and finance are subjects destined to curse any library with cobwebs, there are just as many—or more—who know better. Who can forget the cry of 'taxation without representation,' with its undeniable proof that economic forces give birth to nations?

There are many original and groundbreaking works in the field to occupy the collector. Surely no economic work proved more influential than Adam Smith's *The Wealth of Nations*, "the first and greatest classic of modern economic thought" (PMM). Collecting important editions of this work is of course worthwhile, yet Smith's is not a lonely genius; the collector in this area of classic works will find much notable company.

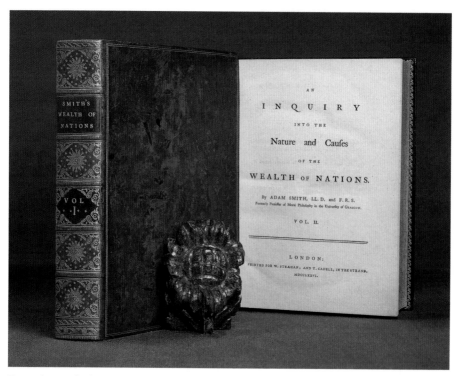

First edition of Adam Smith's *Wealth of Nations*, 1776

In addition to Adam Smith's fundamental classic, eighteenth-century debates over laissez-faire, rational self-interest, mercantilism and the economics of social policy produced many brilliant, if contentious, voices. Among these, the interested collector might wisely invest in the writings of Malthus, in de Mandeville's *The Fable of the Bees*, in de Moivre's writings on probability theory, or in the highly influential proposals of Alexander Hamilton that are found in his reports as Secretary of the Treasury.

Debates over the best or wisest economic and business choices continued into the nineteenth century with the theoretical sophistication of David Ricardo's 1817 treatise *On the Principles of Political Economy* and its influence on John Stuart Mill, the revolutionary theories of Karl Marx, Charles Babbage's studies on industry and the cultural analyses of Henry Mayhew, Charles Mackay and Thorstein Veblen. It was also the end of the nineteenth century that brought the first stirrings of the neoclassical school in the work of Alfred Marshall.

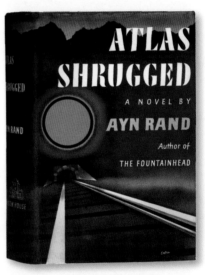

With the turn into the twentieth century, economic theories and business practices were freshly explored, with significant consequence, in the writings of leading thinkers such as Benjamin Graham, Irving Fisher, Frederich Hayek, Ludwig von Mises, Milton Friedman, and, certainly, in the works of John Maynard Keynes, whose *General Theory of Employment* ranks with Smith's classic as one of the giants in the field.

First edition of *Atlas Shrugged*

The book collector with a passion for the drama of this intriguing field has many options to explore. A collection might engage the writings and debate around a single author or economic theory, or it could, with great reward, follow the impact of an economic school into historical, literary or artistic classics, such as Ayn Rand's *Atlas Shrugged*.

ECONOMICS

Illuminated manuscript leaf from a French *Book of Hours,* circa 1475

RELIGION

One cannot ignore the Bible's tremendous influence on world thought and literature. The Bible, of course, was the first book ever printed, and while a Gutenberg Bible of 1455 is no longer a realistic goal for private collectors, many magnificent editions printed in later centuries are. Although collectors seek Bibles in all languages, from the original Greek to the tongues of Native American tribes, it is the English Bible that looms largest. Each of the many famous editions carries with it a story: the Geneva or "Breeches" Bible (1560), the Bible that Shakespeare would have known; the Douai-Rheims Bible (Old Testament, 1582; New Testament, 1609-10), the first Roman Catholic rendering of the Scriptures into English and the foundation for all subsequent Catholic English Bibles for a century; and, of course, the incomparable King James Bible or "Authorized Version" (1611), which Macaulay praised as "a book, which if everything else in our language should perish, would alone suffice to show the whole extent of its beauty and power."

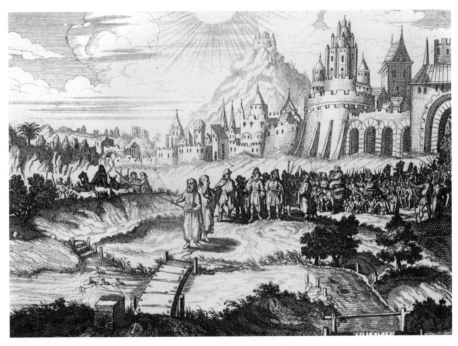

Engraving from the important 1695 Amsterdam Haggadah

Illuminated initial from an incunable Latin Bible , 1480

Many English Bibles were bound together with perhaps the other most influential work of piety in the language, the magisterial Book of Common Prayer. Born of Thomas Cranmer's desire for liturgical texts upon which all of Europe's Protestant, English-speaking churches could agree, the beautiful and dignified language of the Book of Common Prayer, first issued in 1549, has made a considerable impact upon not only ecclesiastical practice but also literature in English. William Reed Huntingdon wrote of it, "There is that in some of [the prayers] which as it has lasted since the days when Roman emperors were sitting on their thrones, so will it last while man continues what he is, a praying creature."

Many fine collections focus on Jewish history and heritage, often with an exquisite Haggadah serving as centerpiece. For centuries, the Haggadah has preserved the elements and essential spirit of the Passover Seder; each edition has its own tale to tell, beyond the story of the Israelites' redemption from slavery that is printed on its pages. Judaica collectors also seek out a wide variety of other material, including Hebrew prayer books, texts about the formation of the modern state of Israel and celebrated books by Jewish authors on religious and cultural subjects. Some collectors preserve for posterity documents that bear witness to anti-Semitism, the Shoah and its aftermath.

Great collections can be built around important sacred texts as old as the Qu'ran (Koran) or as recent as the *Book of Mormon*. They may highlight such celebrated theologians and philosophers as Augustine, Thomas Aquinas, Maimonides, John Calvin or Moses Mendelssohn. Regardless of focus, religious and spiritual collections all reflect in some way humanity's timeless yearning for transcendence.

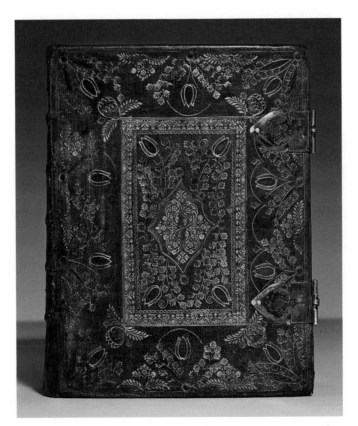

Splendidly bound 1685 King James Bible and Book of Common Prayer

RELIGION

SPORT

Chief Justice Earl Warren remarked, "I always turn to the sports page first, which records people's accomplishments. The front page has nothing but man's failures." Collectors of the literature of sport find inspiration in pages that record historic physical and athletic triumphs.

Sir Edmund Hillary's ascent of Mount Everest is among the most towering of those triumphs. On May 29, 1953, he and Sherpa guide Tenzing Norgay became the first to reach the planet's highest point. Informative and exciting books by and about this pioneering mountaineer include Sir John Hunt's *The Ascent of Everest* (1953), the official account of the expedition.

Not everyone can climb mountains, but almost every American has swung a bat at a ball at least once. Albert Spalding, who would be widely regarded after his death as the "father" of baseball, wrote an early history of the sport in 1911. Collectors also seek signed copies of books by such legends as Babe Ruth, Joe DiMaggio, Jackie

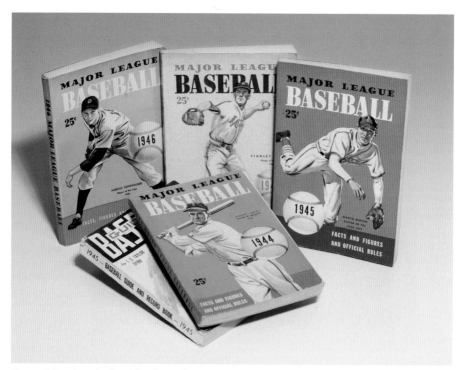

First edition baseball guides from the 1940s

Robinson and Mickey Mantle. The allure of the ballpark can be felt in fiction as well: Bernard Malamud's *The Natural* (1952), Mark Harris' *Bang the Drum Slowly* (1956) and W.P. Kinsella's *Shoeless Joe* (1982) are among the favorites of baseball aficionados. Collectors build baseball libraries for the same reason "people will come" to that field of dreams of Kinsella's book: "The one constant through all the years has been baseball… This game reminds us of all that once was good and could be again."

A large literature for golf has emerged over the years. The first instructional book appeared in 1886—Horace G. Hutchinson's *Hints on the Game of Golf*—and golf titles have been appearing regularly ever since, including works by Bobby Jones, Walter Hagen, Ben Hogan and Arnold Palmer.

Lithograph from Johnson's
Forest, Lake and River, 1902,
an angling classic

Perhaps the most famous sporting book of all, however, is one of the oldest: Izaak Walton and James Cotton's *The Compleat Angler*. First published in 1653, the work is at once a practical guide for fishermen and, arguably, the best long prose-pastoral in English. Along with the Bible and the works of Shakespeare, the *Angler* is, according to some sources, one of the three most frequently published books in the language.

Aquatint of the famous Epsom Derby, circa 1830

MUSIC

Collectors of landmark musical scores enter the worlds of Mozart, Haydn, Bach, Puccini, Mendelssohn, Beethoven, Gershwin and other brilliant composers whose works continue to thrill us. Music collecting is not confined to musicologists or academics; it is neither difficult nor arcane but an area with enormous intrinsic appeal.

Compared to other printed works, musical scores require greater skill and cost to produce. As a result, comparatively fewer works are published, and in comparatively smaller editions. In the past, a work would often have been produced in only a few hand-written scribal copies to be rented out by the publishing house to orchestras or other performers. Only later, after proving to be enduringly popular, would a work be engraved and printed. Indeed, until the end of the nineteenth century, it was not unusual for a music publisher to simultaneously employ scribes, engravers and lithographers, circulating works in all forms depending on their popularity. Thus printed music is often scarce because it was essentially scarce from the beginning, only produced for a limited, musically literate section of society. More

First editions of scores by Beethoven

so than with literary publishing, however, the appeal of music crosses national and linguistic borders.

As in other branches of collecting, "firsts" of various kinds are prized. Many collectors gravitate toward full scores that give instrumental parts for the whole ensemble. Others prefer to collect arrangements for piano and voice. "Piano-vocal" scores of operas were simpler to print than orchestral scores, and in the pre-recording age had a ready market among recreational music-makers: these arrangements were often published years before the full score. The piano-vocal score

"Do not think that the old music is outmoded. Just as a beautiful true word can never be outmoded, so a beautiful piece of true music." —Schumann

of Mozart's *Don Giovanni*, for example, was printed in 1791, while the full score was not printed for another ten years.

For composers from the early years of the nineteenth century or before, "lifetime editions," published while the composer was still alive, are among the most desirable scores. This is especially the case when collecting Mozart since many of his full scores were printed only after his death. For example, *The Magic Flute* was composed in 1791, the last year of Mozart's life, but the full score was not published until 1814.

As with literature, inscribed or signed copies are greatly prized. But with music, there is an expanded opportunity for interesting and valuable association copies: a work can be almost as strongly associated with a conductor or a performer as it can with its composer. A full score owned by a noted conductor might be of great interest, for example, particularly if it contained his annotations or other evidence of his use. A copy of Verdi's *Requiem Mass* signed by the composer is, naturally, valuable, but is particularly fascinating if it is also signed by Teresa Stolz and Maria Waldmann, the two female soloists in the Mass' premiere performance. Additionally, a composer will sometimes inscribe a work with bars of music in addition to words; over the years we have seen works inscribed in this manner by such a diverse group of composers as Claude Debussy, George Gershwin, Jules Massenet, Giacomo Puccini, Maurice Ravel and Igor Stravinsky.

The twentieth century introduces new possibilities for the music collector, from albums to sheet music to printed programs and other unusual items. Just as with literature, on occasion publishers would issue sumptuous deluxe signed limited editions of printed music, such as Cole Porter's *Red Hot and Blue* (1936) and Gershwin's *Porgy and Bess* (1935). Scores of musical works are as diverse as the vast world of music. From baroque composers of the seventeenth century to impressionistic composers of the twentieth, from sacred chorales to scandalous operas, from symphonies to sonatas, the world of music entices the collector.

1801 first edition of the full score of Mozart's *Don Giovanni*

Format

O ne of the mysteries encountered by the beginning collector is a series of abbreviations used to describe a book's size: 4to, 8vo, 12mo, etc. Words such as *folio*, *quarto*, *octavo* and *duodecimo* began to regularly appear in an emerging book trade during the sixteenth century. *Folio* is Latin for leaf, *quarto* means one-quarter or fourth, and *octavo* means one-eighth or eighth.

Terms such as octavo or folio are, in effect, a record of a book's evolution from single sheet to printed page. They indicate how many times an original printed sheet was folded after printing in order to produce the book's printed leaves and pages. When printing, an even number of pages (4, 8, 16, 32) is laid out and printed on a single sheet. That sheet is then folded, with the pages in their correct order, and the format term helps indicate how many times an original sheet has been folded into leaves.

Folio, for example, is a term that tells us a sheet was folded once and has two leaves. Each of the leaves has a front, or *recto*, and a reverse, or *verso*. These two sides, or

Elephant Folio	14" x 23"
Folio	12" x 19"
Quarto	9 ½" x 12"
Royal Octavo	6 ½" x 10"
Octavo	6" x 9"
Duodecimo (12mo)	5" x 7 ½"
Sixteenmo (16mo)	4" x 6 ¾"

(Measurements are approximate.)

leaves, produce four printed pages. In a *quarto* (4to, 4°), the original sheet has been folded twice, that is, folded once in half, then in half again. This results in four leaves (each 1/4 the size of the original sheet) and eight pages. Similarly an *octavo* (8vo, 8°) has been folded three times, creating eight leaves and sixteen pages.

Paper comes in different sizes, though. Because of that, the term for a book's format does not necessarily convert to inches or centimeters. After all, format is primarily a record of the folds used to produce leaves, then pages, and a book's actual size and shape might depend more on that sheet's original size than the number of its folds. Because there are so many paper sizes, these terms and their measurements can never be absolutely consistent or exact. These descriptive terms are used as approximations of size.

Format

Book Production

The process of book production in earlier times began with the laying out of individual blocks of type (or formes) by the printer. Early books were not often paginated, so to ensure that each page's block of text would be properly arranged, a *catchword* was often placed at the foot of each page that matched the first word on the next. These *catchwords* helped the printer ensure that the proper order of formes would be locked into a larger frame known as a *chase* when this was printed in its entirety on one side of a large sheet of paper. The same process would be followed with the reverse side of the same large sheet. Then the printed sheet would be folded in half one or more times into a gathering of leaves, each with pages constituting the leaf's *recto* ("right" side) and *verso* ("reverse" side).

According to John Carter, the "sheet is the printer's unit, the leaf the bibliographer's; the gathering is the binder's." In other words, the printer always began with a large flat sheet. It was the binder who assembled a sequence of gatherings, or folded, printed sheets, arranging them in their proper order with the help of the *signature* code that usually consisted of a small capital letter printed in the lower margin of the first page of each gathering (or sometimes on the next few leaves as well). To prevent a confusion of "i" and "j," or "u" and "v," one or both of these pairs (along with a "w") were often omitted from the signature alphabet. It is also worth knowing that it has become common to call each gathering a *signature*. Once the gatherings, or *signatures*, were arranged into the proper sequence by the binder, they would be stitched, stapled or glued together.

Over time the bibliographer needed a way to identify a book's format, so it was decided that, in this instance, format follows leaf. A *quarto* (or "fourth"), for example, became the term used for a book composed of signatures of two folds and four leaves: an *octavo* ("eighth") one with signatures of three folds and eight leaves, and so on. Given that each leaf has two sides, a gathering of four leaves will produce eight pages, a gathering of eight leaves, sixteen pages.

With the book finally formed, its parts stacked, sealed and delivered, signatures and pages in their proper order, every catchword properly sequenced, bibliographers devised a shorthand system for assessing the number and order of signatures in a printed book, what is called its *collation*. A formula of letters and numbers was devised to record the arrangement of pages. This tells us when all the pages of an edition are present and permits an economical means of comparing several copies of the same printing, a method that became especially useful for books printed without pagination. A *collation* also lets us know when the occasional page or section is missing or rearranged (even though the book is complete, leaves may be out of place); it also indicates when there are extra leaves or cancels.

Several other terms used in book production may also prove useful for the book collector. A *cancel*, for example, is used to describe both a part of a book that has been removed and its replacement. The most common form of a cancel is the single-leaf cancel, but a cancel might be any size. It may appear as a tiny piece of paper with "the" printed on it, pasted on a page over an incorrect "this." If, during the printing process, a larger error is discovered, an entire sheet or leaf might be removed, to be replaced by a newly printed section. Though it may be difficult to readily identify a cancel, this practice has, at times, proved invaluable in distinguishing between the stages of a book's production, or between the states of an edition. *Errata* are reports of errors found after a book has been printed. An *errata slip*, for example, might be printed and *tipped in* (attached with a thin line of glue close to the inner hinge). The presence or absence of an errata slip may provide useful information to the collector.

As we've just seen, elements may be added to a book after it was printed and bound. Laying down a very thin strip of adhesive to the inner edge of a page closest to the book's hinge, then attaching the tipped-in leaf often accomplishes this. Small errata slips are often found tipped-in at the preliminaries. If additional materials such as maps or extra engravings have been tipped in to a particular copy, it is called *extra-illustrated*.

Frequently Asked Questions

1. WHAT MAKES A BOOK RARE?

Rarity is not simply dependent on age or scarcity. A rare book is one that is important, desirable, and scarce. An important book is one that had a profound effect when printed and which continues to exert influence.

A number of factors can affect the scarcity of a book, including printing history, the number of copies printed or sold, the quality of the paper and binding (the more fragile the book, the less likely it will survive in fine condition), any controversy surrounding the book, its popularity (or lack of it) and its genre. For example, children's books, read and handled by children, are difficult to find intact; early herbals, law books, cookbooks and Bibles often bear the marks of practical use as well.

2. WHAT ARE THE DIFFERENCES BETWEEN *EDITION, PRINTING, ISSUE* AND *STATE?*

An edition includes all copies printed from the same plates or setting of type without substantial change. The *first edition* consists of all the copies printed from the first setting of type and is the first public appearance of the text in book form. Any *edition* can appear in multiple *printings*, and each printing includes all of the copies produced from the same plates or setting of type at a given time (for example, an edition may include 1000 copies, 500 printed in November, the additional 500 printed in January from the same setting of type).

States are created when publishers make minor corrections, alterations or additions to the text, illustrations, dust jacket or other elements of a book before publication, such as when a typographical error is corrected during the course of printing, or the caption is changed on an illustration. *Issues* are created intentionally by the publisher to produce copies that differ from the rest in some way and are treated as a separate unit, such as in the case of a *large-paper issue*, or when a new title page is substituted after publication.

While priority among the different states of a first edition often cannot be determined, a first issue always precedes a second issue. In some cases, collectors might prefer a later issue. For example, the second issue of Walt Whitman's *Drum Taps* includes the poet's moving homage to the fallen president Abraham Lincoln, "When Lilacs Last in the Dooryard Bloom'd," a poem not included in the first issue, which was prepared before Lincoln's death.

Sometimes, a statement of "first edition" needs to be qualified. The phrase "first American edition," for instance, indicates that the book was first published in another country and this is its first appearance in America. The "first English edition" is a book's first appearance in Britain, while the "first edition in English" is the first English-language edition of a book that first appeared in a different language. Some books are issued by the publisher in two forms: *a first trade edition*, the mass-produced copies for sale in stores, and a special or *limited edition*, produced in small quantities, often in a different binding or issued with a page signed by the author (called a *signed limited edition*).

First edition of Jane Austen's *Pride and Prejudice*, 1813

3. HOW DO YOU DETERMINE IF A BOOK IS A FIRST EDITION?

There is no one standard way to determine edition; it differs among books. Many publishers do not consistently identify their first editions (this is especially true of books printed prior to the twentieth century). Those that do identify first editions use various methods: some publishers print the words "First Edition" or "First Printing" on the copyright page, or they might use a special symbol or series of numbers to indicate edition. For many works, individual author bibliographies must be consulted in order to be sure that a book is a true first edition. Bibliographers study an author's printed works and detail the characteristics of the books themselves, including binding, typography, and content. The variations they record—the color of a cloth binding, a misspelling on a particular page, or a photograph, award notice or price on a dust jacket—are known as *points*. *Points* can be essential to determining the edition, issue or state of a particular copy. Cataloguers work from an extensive library of reference material and check carefully to determine the edition (and issue or state, if appropriate) of any book.

4. HOW MANY COPIES WERE PRINTED IN EACH FIRST EDITION? HOW DO YOU KNOW?

Again, it depends on the book. Obviously, a limited first edition is printed in a specific number, generally noted on the limitation page. In other cases, publisher's records may state the number of copies printed of a first edition, or an author may mention the size of a first edition in correspondence. For the majority of first editions, however, the exact number of copies is not known.

5. DO LATER EDITIONS EVER HAVE ANY VALUE, OR SHOULD I ALWAYS LOOK FOR FIRST EDITIONS?

The very general rule in book collecting is that the first edition of a particular work is the most desirable, but there are numerous exceptions. This is particularly so in the case of non-fiction titles, such as historical works and narratives of travel and exploration. In these areas, a second or later edition may be preferable because of additional material, including maps, illustrations or important information not contained in the first. Later editions may also be greatly improved in format and organization over a first edition. Indeed, bibliographers will often designate a "best edition": that is, an edition preferred for its superior organization and content. In literature, there may also be a preference for a later edition: for example, Elizabeth Barrett Browning's "Sonnets From the Portuguese" appears in the second edition of her *Poems*, not in the first edition.

In the case of some important and early works, a first edition may be nearly unobtainable and thus later editions are often a collector's only recourse. Similarly, some collectors prefer collecting first editions in English. There are several reasons for such a focus: true first editions in the original language may be unobtainable, an English-speaking collector may prefer to collect books he or she can read, or a particular work's impact upon its publication in English may rival the impact of its first publication.

Collectors of modern first editions generally want to acquire copies as close as possible to the work's first appearance. Some exceptions do apply: a beautifully bound set of an author's works can complement a collection of first editions, or a later edition of a favorite work signed by the author or with a wonderful association can be highly desirable.

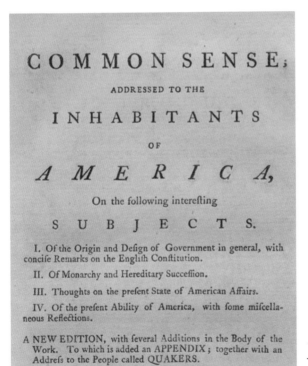

1776 printing of Thomas Paine's *Common Sense*

6. WHY IS THE DUST JACKET SO IMPORTANT TO MODERN FIRST EDITIONS?

Dust jackets or dust wrappers were originally designed to protect a book in transit until it reached the safety of an owner's library. The first recorded use of a dust jacket dates to the mid-nineteenth century, but because of their utilitarian beginnings, they were generally discarded and very early jackets, with few exceptions, do not survive.

The early twentieth century, however, saw dust jackets elevated from simple coverings to art forms and promotional aids integral to the book. Because collectors of modern first editions generally want a copy as close as possible to its first appearance in every way, most prefer a dust jacket when obtainable (some dust jackets are exceptionally scarce, such as those of *The Great Gatsby* and *The Sun Also Rises*).

As with books, condition is essential to the value of a dust jacket. Made of paper, they are fragile by nature, and though no longer designed only for protection, they remain the book's first defense against sunlight, humidity, handling, dust, and other stresses. Thus, they can show substantial wear: chipping, fading, darkening, staining and tears. They are still often discarded, and many are more fragile and prone to wear than others (for example, they may be light colored and show soiling quite easily, or made of a particularly fragile paper and prone to chipping or fading). Just as the difference in value between a modern first edition with a jacket and a copy without can be considerable, so can the difference in value between a poor jacket and fine or near-fine jacket.

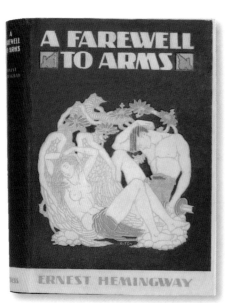

First edition of *A Farewell to Arms* in the scarce original dust jacket

Original etching from Goya's *Tauromaquia*

7. HOW IMPORTANT IS CONDITION?

The importance of condition in book collecting cannot be underestimated. Copies in exceptional condition are at a premium, and the oft-repeated adage is that a collector should buy the best possible copy that he or she can afford. Often, that means a copy in "fine" condition. But it is also important to keep in mind the particular title, its printing history, and its scarcity. A very modern signed first edition might be obtainable in "mint" condition, but a mid-nineteenth-century narrative of Western exploration printed in America will probably not survive without at least some foxing or wear or repair to the binding. With very scarce books, a "very good" copy may be the best a collector can hope to find.

8. HOW IMPORTANT IS PROVENANCE?

The specific history of a copy from the printing press to your shelves is its *provenance*. Provenance can be determined by a variety of indicators, including bookplates, owner signatures and gift inscriptions. Sometimes the provenance has been recorded within the volume or in separate records. While the provenance can sometimes add to a book's value (if it belonged to a famous historical figure or came from an esteemed library), in most cases it simply adds to the interest of the book. Unfortunately, the vast majority of books do not have a traceable provenance as they have been passed from owner to owner throughout the years without note.

Of the variations of provenance, those copies that can be directly linked to their authors generally do have enhanced value (often considerable). Presentation (given by the writer to someone) and association copies

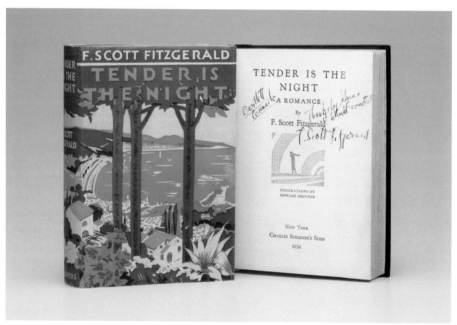

First edition of Fitzgerald's *Tender is the Night*, inscribed by him to a fellow Hollywood screenwriter

(belonging to someone connected with the author) are usually more valuable than regular copies, and in the case of presentation copies, the length and content of the presentation is important. Consider, for instance, this inscription in a first edition presentation copy of *The Sun Also Rises*: "To Sylvia with great affection—Ernest Hemingway, Paris, November 1926." Hemingway was a faithful patron of Sylvia Beach's bookshop, Shakespeare and Company, a key gathering place for the "lost generation" of writers. The association is extraordinary, representing an enormous increase in value of an already most desirable rarity.

9. DO I NEED TO MAKE SPECIAL PROVISIONS FOR THESE BOOKS IN MY HOME?

In general, books are designed to be read and to last. They should be handled with care and usually require little maintenance, but there are some important guidelines.

Books should be kept in a relatively stable environment, one that is not too hot, too cold, too dry or too damp. Very high humidity can damage books, warping boards and encouraging mold, and should be avoided.

Books must be kept away from direct sunlight, which will destroy leather bindings and fade dust jackets. A protective acid-free clear mylar jacket should be kept on all dust jackets. Sometimes, with more fragile books, a protective box or slipcase can be made. It is also recommended that periodically, perhaps once a year, some leather bindings be dressed with special leather dressing and gently buffed to keep the leather supple.

"Books are the treasured wealth of the world and the fit inheritance of generations and nations." Henry David Thoreau

List of References

GENERAL GUIDES

THOMAS, Alan G. *Great Books and Book Collectors.* A large-format book with almost 300 illustrations, including 40 color plates, that traces the development of books from the manuscripts of the medieval period to the growth of private presses in the twentieth century and profiles major collectors and their libraries.

PORTER, Catherine. *Miller's Collecting Books.* Full of color illustrations and suggestions on how to get started in various areas of collecting, this is an excellent guide for both beginners and those more experienced in book collecting who wish to expand their horizons.

Once you've become enthusiastic about book collecting in general, the next decision is what to collect. The following works can help you form a wish list for creating an extraordinary library. These books entertain while informing the reader about the influence of books throughout history.

CARTER, John and **MUIR**, Percy, editors. *Printing and the Mind of Man.* "PMM" is based on the catalogue for a 1963 exhibition, perhaps the greatest exhibition ever of printed works, encompassing 464 of the most influential works ever printed. Assigning greatness is always arbitrary, but a PMM citation is as close to an official imprimatur as one will find.

OLMERT, Michael. *The Smithsonian Book of Books.* A lavishly illustrated work focusing largely on the history of great books.

GENERAL GUIDES

KENT, Henry W. *Bibliographical Notes on One Hundred Books Famous in English Literature.* Better known as the "Grolier 100," this group was originally gathered together for an exhibition at the Grolier Club in New York in 1903, and it ranges from a 1478 edition of Chaucer to John Greenleaf Whittier's *Snow-Bound*, published in 1866. Some helpful bibliographical information is included with each work, as well as a short summary.

CONNOLLY, Cyril. *The Modern Movement.* Yet another list of 100 books, these are the key books in defining the Modern Movement from 1880 to 1950, which "began as a revolt against the bourgeois in France, the Victorians in England, the Puritanism and materialism of America." The famed critic states his case for "books with outstanding originality and richness of texture and with the spark of rebellion alight, books which aspire to be works of art."

Detail from the first edition of Webster's *American Dictionary*, 1828

The following are a few of the most frequently cited general references in the field of rare and antiquarian books, so well-known that they are usually referred to on a one-name basis such as "Sabin" or "Allibone." While only an advanced collector would need these in his or her personal library, it is good to be familiar with them and know what they contain. Finding a work in one of these references is no guarantee of importance, but it is often one of the only sources for information on the work, and in the case of the collection catalogues (such as Streeter or Abbey) it is reassuring to know that the book you are seeking has been thought worthy of inclusion in one of the greatest libraries ever assembled. All these works have their limitations and idiosyncrasies, but all are also among the most complete references in their fields, remarkable for the amount of information they contain and for the effort that went into completing them. The epigraph attached to Sabin's work could well be applied to any of these: "A painfull work it is, I'll assure you, and more than difficult, wherein what toyle has been taken, as no man thinketh so no man believeth, but he hath made the triall."

AMERICANA REFERENCES

SABIN, Joseph. *A Dictionary of Books relating to America, from its Discovery to the Present Time.* Originally published in parts beginning in 1867. Contains over 100,000 works published in or about America, with a brief bibliographical entry and an indication of the libraries or personal collections where the work can be found. A remarkably comprehensive listing up to the date of publication. Sabin commented, "Had the magnitude and extreme difficulty of the undertaking been presented to my mind in full proportion at the outset, I should never have attempted it."

HOWES, Wright. *U.S.Iana.* (1650-1950). Originally issued in 1954 and revised in 1962. A wide-ranging bibliographic work, but with a sharper focus than Sabin, limiting itself to works on "human activities" in the continental United States. Howes also dismisses some "common" or insignificant works: "No mature collector buys material in that category; and books unfit for purchase are surely unfit for admittance into a selective bibliography. An unweeded garden is close kin to a jungle!"

STREETER, Thomas Winthrop. *The Celebrated Collection of Americana Formed by the Late Thomas Winthrop Streeter*. A truly remarkable catalogue of the sale of Streeter's collection by the Parke-Bernet Galleries in 1966, published in seven well-illustrated volumes plus an index. Over 4,000 items in all areas of Americana.

FIELD, Thomas W. *An Essay Towards an Indian Bibliography*. Published in 1873. A catalogue of Field's library of over 1,700 works on Native Americans, enhanced by the often-opinionated comments attached to many entries.

WHEAT, Carl I. *Mapping the Transmississippi West, 1540-1861*. This wonderful and comprehensive five-volume reference, originally published in 1957, chronicles the development of maps of the Western frontier. It is richly illustrated with hundreds of reproductions, often full-size, of the most important manuscript and printed maps. Naturally many of the landmark books of western exploration included maps—Mackenzie, Lewis and Clark, Fremont, to name a few—and Wheat carefully evaluates their impact.

ENGLISH LITERATURE REFERENCES

ALLIBONE, S. Austin. *A Critical Dictionary of English Literature and British and American Authors Living and Deceased From the Earliest Accounts to the Latter Half of the Nineteenth Century*. Born in Philadelphia in 1816, Allibone produced the first volume of this massive work in 1858 and the final one in 1870. It contains quotations, often lengthy, from critical judgments on over 46,000 authors, with forty classified indexes of subjects.

POLLARD, A. W. and **REDGRAVE**, G. R. *A Short-title Catalogue of Books Printed in England, Scotland, and Ireland and of English Books Printed Abroad 1475-1640*. First published in 1927. Popularly known as "STC," this work was first compiled by Redgrave, an architect, engineer and art historian and Pollard, Keeper of Printed Books at the British Museum, who warned all users that "it is a dangerous work for anyone to handle lazily." Nevertheless, the bibliographic information contained is invaluable. A second edition, revised and enlarged, was issued between 1976 and 1991.

ENGLISH LITERATURE

WING, Donald. *Short-title Catalogue of Books Printed in England, Scotland, Ireland, Wales, and British America and of English books Printed in Other Countries 1641-1700.* Wing, a Yale librarian, eventually filled fifty-two shoeboxes with cataloguing information from Yale, as well as from various other libraries he had visited, (he was often locked in for the night while doing his research). Copies of his findings were circulated to other major libraries, which added their holdings to this catalogue.

LOWNDES, William Thomas. *The Bibliographer's Manual of English Literature.* First published in 1834. Lowndes, the son and grandson of booksellers, began to compile

Charles Dickens

this work in 1820. "Though the first systematic work of its kind in England, it brought Lowndes neither notice nor money. He passed the latter part of his life in drudgery and complete poverty" (DNB). Though with fewer contemporary critical citations than Allibone, Lowndes' observations are astute, and he gives more attention to the needs of collectors. A revised edition was issued in 1857.

BATESON, F. W. *The Cambridge Bibliography of English Literature.* An offshoot of the great *Cambridge History of English Literature*, this Bibliography is conceived along the same lines as Lowndes, but it is both more accurate and more complete, a listing of major and minor English literary works.

OTHER REFERENCES

ABBEY, J. R. *Travel in Aquatint and Lithography 1170-1860 from the Library of J. R. Abbey.* First printed in 1956. A wonderful library catalogue of illustrated travel works from the collection of J. R. Abbey, one of the greatest English book collectors of his time.

BRUCCOLI, Matthew J. and **CLARK**, C. E. Frazer, Jr. *First Printings of American Authors.* 1977. You have to love a reference work whose poetic preface states, "What springs mingle in the urge to collect books is as impossible to distinguish as what song the sirens sang." Even better is the bibliographic material on hundreds of major American writers accompanied by reproductions of original dust jackets.

COX, Edward Godfrey. *A Reference Guide to the Literature of Travel.* "Convinced," as he said, "that no man can ever be a bibliographer," Cox set himself to what he saw as the less demanding task of listing "in chronological order, from the earliest date ascertainable down to and including the year 1800, all the books on foreign travels, voyages and descriptions printed in Great Britain."

DARLOW, T. H. and **MOULE**, H. F. *Historical Catalogue of the Printed Editions of Holy Scripture in the Library of the British and Foreign Bible Society.* Originally published in 1903, this is the most complete listing of editions of the Bible. A revised and updated edition of the English-language section was published by A. S. Herbert in 1968.

GARRISON, Fielding and **MORTON**, Leslie. *Morton's Medical Bibliography.* Leslie Morton's comprehensive bibliography of texts illustrating the history of Medicine, greatly expanded from an outline of sources published by Fielding Garrison in 1935. While the work is mostly Morton's, this important reference is still referred to and cited as Garrison & Morton.

HILL, Kenneth. *The Hill Collection of Pacific Voyages.* "Almost any volume in this collection has the magical ability to turn a reader into an explorer." Detailed catalogue of Hill's renowned and comprehensive collection of published works related to exploration of the Pacific Ocean and the continents and islands it touches, from the sixteenth to the nineteenth centuries. A fantastic collection, including the voyages of Anson, Cook, Bligh, Vancouver, Drake, Humboldt, and many others.

MISCELLANEOUS

Types of Bindings

ORIGINAL CLOTH

Beginning around 1830, publishers began to issue their books in more permanent bindings covered in cloth. These bindings ranged from plain cloth covers with gilt lettering on the spine only to elaborate gift bindings pictorially decorated in gilt or blind or both.

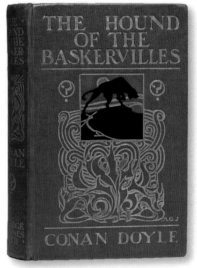

First edition of *Hound of the Baskervilles*, in the original cloth-gilt binding

DUST JACKETS

Dust jackets or dust wrappers were originally designed to protect a book in transit until it reached the safety of an owner's library. The first recorded use of a dust jacket dates to the mid-nineteenth century, but because of their utilitarian beginnings, they were generally discarded; very early jackets, with few exceptions, have not survived. In the early twentieth century dust jackets evolved from simple coverings to evocative works of art integral to the book.

First edition of Harper Lee's *To Kill a Mockingbird*, in the original dust jacket

ORIGINAL CLOTH AND DUST JACKETS

ORIGINAL BOARDS

As an increasing number of books began to be published and sold in the 1700s and through to the early 1830s, printers and publishers (often the same individual or bookseller) began selling their books in "boards," what are today called "original boards." Here the text block was printed and sewn together, then covered by blue, gray, or marbled paper-covered pasteboards, with a paper (or sometimes calf) spine and perhaps a hand-written or printed-paper label. Like the plain dust jackets issued with books in the late nineteenth century, these simple bindings were intended to be disposable. A book's eighteenth century owner would take his purchase to a binder who would usually replace the original boards with a permanent binding. Books still in original boards are considered to be quite desirable by collectors.

First edition of Gass' 1807 account of the Lewis and Clark expedition, in original boards

ORIGINAL WRAPPERS

In the eighteenth century slim volumes like pamphlets, periodicals or serials would be sewn together and covered in paper, often of the same stock or possibly of heavier marbled paper. Paper wrappers were designed to give the text block some protection before the purchaser would have it bound; these are the most fragile of bindings and are infrequently found intact. Later in the nineteenth century publishers began issuing periodicals and fiction—such as Dickens' and Thackeray's novels—in wrappers of bright colors, with illustrations calling attention to the contents and advertisements on the rear wrapper for the publisher's other titles or for other companies' products; these were the forerunners of today's paperbacks.

1774 Philadelphia printing of the
Extracts from the First Continental Congress,
in original wrappers

**ORIGINAL BOARDS
AND WRAPPERS**

CALF

Bindings made from calf hide are the most frequently seen leather coverings. Such bindings have a smooth surface with no identifiable grain. The natural tone of a calf binding is light brown, but can be dyed almost any color. The following terms are often associated with calf bindings:

DICED: a decorative design of diamonds or squares that has been scored onto the leather.

MARBLED: stained with a diluted acid to produce the effect of swirling hues.

MOTTLED: a random design on calfskin produced by sponging it with acid or dyes.

PANELED: a rectangular space on a cover or spine, often framed by gilt or plain ruled lines tooled into the leather.

POLISHED: calfskin polished to a smooth, reflective finish.

REVERSED: binding with the inner side of the skin facing outward.

SPANISH: a process, originating in Spain, of using red and green acid dye to stain brilliant flecks of color in the binding.

SPECKLED: leather treated with acid to form patterns of small dark spots or specks.

TREE CALF: a highly polished calf binding that originated in the late 18th century in which the leather has been stained to produce a dark tree-like pattern along the front and rear boards.

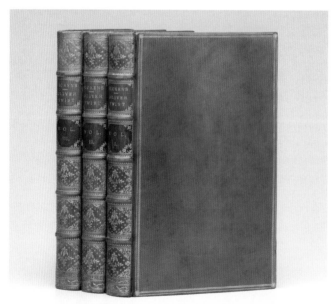

First edition of Dickens' *Oliver Twist*, bound in full polished calf-gilt

MOROCCO

Made of goatskin and often dyed in strong, bold colors, morocco bindings are known for both their beauty and durability. Morocco bindings appeared in Europe in the sixteenth century and in England in the late seventeenth century. The following terms are often associated with morocco bindings.

CRUSHED: the surface of the leather is flattened by ironing, pressing or rolling, producing a surface with no discernible grain.

LEVANT: a large-grain morocco binding, usually highly polished, considered the most elegant of morocco bindings.

NIGER: a flexible, rugged binding originating in West Africa that has a soft finish, with a subtle grain achieved through hand-rubbing.

STRAIGHT-GRAIN: very popular in the early nineteenth century, this type of morocco binding is produced by moistening the goatskin, then giving the leather an artificial graining of roughly parallel lines.

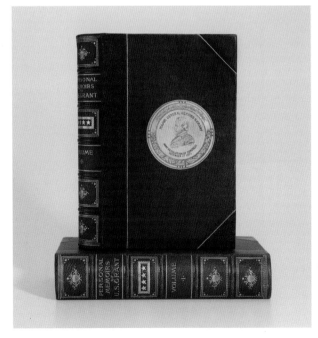

First edition of Grant's *Memoirs*, in the original publisher's three-quarter morocco binding

MOROCCO

COSWAY-STYLE BINDINGS

Richly tooled bindings with miniature paintings embedded in their covers, Cosway bindings were first created in 1902 by the famous Rivière bindery. Rivière employed Miss C.B. Currie with instructions to imitate the delicate watercolor style of the renowned nineteenth-century miniaturist Richard Cosway. These miniatures, mostly portraits and often on ivory, were set into the covers or doublures of fine bindings and protected by thin panes of glass.

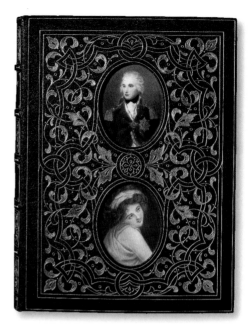

Elaborately gilt-decorated full morocco Cosway-style binding, featuring inset portraits of Lord Nelson and Lady Hamilton

VELLUM

From medieval times onward, this specially treated calfskin has been used for writing and printing on as well as for binding. Many medieval manuscripts, for instance, were written on vellum. In later centuries, vellum has been used to bind books. In the early twentieth century, publishers issued deluxe illustrated gift editions bound in elaborately gilt-decorated vellum.

First edition of Aubrey Beardsley's illustrated *Morte D'Arthur*, 1893, in full vellum-gilt

COSWAY-STYLE AND VELLUM

JEWELED BINDINGS

Occasionally a binder will decorate the covers of a book with inlaid jewels and fine stones, such as mother-of-pearl, rubies, moonstones, amethysts and turquoise. These elaborate bindings were often designed for exhibitions and frequently incorporate designs in inlaid morocco as well as full morocco doublures, watered silk endpapers and gilt edges.

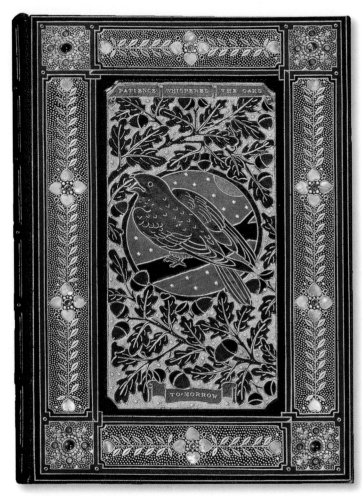

Longfellow's *Evangeline*, in a magnificent jeweled binding by Sangorski and Sutcliffe

JEWELED

Glossary

ANNOTATED: with hand-written notations in the book regarding the text, on blanks or in the margins, usually by an owner who has some sort of association to the text or the author (as opposed to marginalia, where the author of the commentary is unknown, though the comments may be just as copious and/or astute).

AQUATINT: copperplate process by which the plate is "bitten" through exposure to acid. By changing the areas of the plate that are exposed and the length of time the plate is submerged in the acid bath, the engraver can obtain fine and varying shades of gray that closely resemble watercolor washes. Although the name contains the word "tint," this is a black-and-white printing process; aquatint plates are often hand-colored, however.

ARMORIAL: with the owner's coat-of-arms, usually used to refer to bookplates or bindings. An armorial binding can also refer to a book decorated with the coat-of-arms of a member of royalty or of the nobility. Such decoration does not necessarily indicate that the book was in the sovereign's library, however: presentation copies from a queen to visiting dignitaries may have been bound with her arms; likewise the Eikon Basilike of 1649 is often found bearing the arms of the executed Charles I.

ASSOCIATION COPY: copy that belonged to someone connected with the author or the contents of a book.

AUTOGRAPH: adjective meaning hand-written, as in "autograph letter signed"; not used in the book trade as a noun meaning signature.

AUTOGRAPH LETTER SIGNED (ALS): entirely handwritten letter signed by the author.

BLACK-LETTER: heavy Germanic type-faces also known as *gothic*, found frequently in early books, as distinct from the lighter roman or italic typefaces that eventually superseded them.

BOARDS: front and back of a hardcover book, covered in cloth, leather or paper. "Original boards" refers to paper-backed boards used beginning in the latter part of the eighteenth century through the first half of the nineteenth century as temporary protection for books before their purchasers would have them bound. Of particular value to collectors.

BOOKPLATE: label, generally affixed to the front pastedown, identifying a book's owner.

BROADSIDE: sheet printed on one side, typically for public display, usually larger than folio size (a folio being a broadside-size sheet printed on both sides and folded once, to make four pages).

CALF: binding material made from cowhide—versatile, durable, usually tan or brown in color, of smooth texture with no or little apparent grain. Readily marbled ("tree calf"), mottled, diced, colored, polished, tooled in gilt or blind, even scented (known as "russia"). Reverse calf, with a distinctive suede-like texture, is occasionally used.

CANCEL: leaf inserted in place of a leaf removed to correct an error or as a result of censorship; the page removed is called the cancelland. Can also refer to a slip of paper pasted over the changed passage, often then called a cancel slip.

CATCHWORD: first word of the next page placed just below the last line of the preceding page, an obsolete practice. Catchwords were for the printers, not the readers, to ensure that the signatures had been properly folded and stacked; the printer only had to make sure each catchword matched the first word on the following page as he flipped through the text. These are often useful in collating an early printed book in which page numbers are sometimes incorrect or repeated (mispaginated).

CHROMOLITHOGRAPH: lithograph printed in colors, typically more than three. Lithographs printed in black plus only on or two additional colors (usually a muted earth tone and possibly a pale sky tone) are usually referred to as *tinted lithographs* rather than chromolithographs, which are generally vibrantly multicolored and often with gold or silver ink highlights.

COLOPHON: printed note at the end of a text containing information about the printing of the book.

COLLATION: process by which the contents of a book are inspected for completeness, checking against internal evidence, the table of contents and/or plate list, and reference works. Also a shorthand bibliographical description of a book's composition by its leaves and signatures, rather than its pages. A-C^4, for example, would indicate a quarto volume composed of three signatures or gatherings of eight pages each for a total of 24 pages.

CONTEMPORARY: of the period of issue. Can be used to describe a book's binding, if within a decade or two of publication, marks of ownership or marginalia, hand coloring, rubrication, anything done to a text block at roughly the same time as it was issued. *Not to be confused with modern.*

DEDICATION COPY: copy of a book presented by the author to the book's printed dedicatee.

DOCUMENT SIGNED (DS): official or legal document, whether printed and completed in manuscript (i.e., by hand, typically secretarial) or executed entirely by hand, signed by a person of some import.

DOUBLURE: pastedowns made not of paper but of leather or silk, usually decorative.

DUODECIMO (12MO): smaller than an octavo, typically less than six inches tall; smaller formats, such as 24mo and 32mo, are uncommon.

EDITION: print-run from a single setting of type. Depending on demand, any number of printings can be made from a setting of type: a first printing might consist of 1000 copies, for example, followed by a second printing of 2500 copies, followed by a third of 550.

ENDPAPERS: double leaves—plain, colored or decorated—with which a bookbinder covers the insides of the book's boards, therefore not part of the text block. The leaf pasted to the inside of the front board is the *front pastedown*, the leaf following is the *front free endpaper*; the same applies to the *rear pastedown* and *rear free endpaper*.

ENGRAVING: illustration produced by carving or etching lines into a plate of copper or (after 1830) steel; shading is achieved variously by cross-hatching, "biting" the plate with acid (aquatint) or roughing the surface with a rocker (stippling or mezzotint). Ink is poured over the plate, then wiped from the surface, leaving ink only in the recesses made by the engraver's tools; the image is transferred by pressing thick dampened paper against the metal plate with great force, requiring engravings to be printed on a separate stock and separate press from any text.

ERRATA: list of mistakes and corrections noted after printing, often compiled on a separate sheet or slip and inserted into the text block.

EX-LIBRARY MARKINGS: bookplates, blind- or inkstamps, shelf numbers and other indications that a book once belonged to a circulating or institutional library.

EXTRA-ILLUSTRATED: process of inserting illustrations, letters or autographs in addition to those already present in a book, supplied either by the collector or the publisher, to make a more deluxe edition. Also called *grangerized*, after pioneering English publisher James Granger.

FLYLEAVES: additional blank leaves following or preceding the endpapers.

FOLIO: book composed of sheets printed on both sides, folded once, to make two leaves and four pages. Typically above 14 inches tall. *Oblong folios* are produced the same way but bound at the short edge, producing a book typically more than 14 inches deep.

FORE-EDGE: edge of the book furthest from the spine. Occasionally the text of a book will be put into a specialized book press and painted, often with a scene from the book or a landscape, so that the painting is invisible when the book is closed but visible when somebody bends the text and fans the pages—known as a *fore-edge painting*.

FOXING: light brown spots that naturally appear on some papers as they age.

HALF TITLE: leaf preceding the title page that bears the book's title, originally used to identify the unbound text block. The book's binder would often remove and discard the half title at the time of binding. Remaining half-titles are always of interest to collectors.

HAND-COLORED: illustration that has been colored by hand, typically with watercolors, at or shortly after the time of publication. Before color printing processes were widely available, hand-coloring was the most economically feasible way of producing illustrations in color; the coloring could range from finely rendered paintings with rich palettes to a few brushstrokes of color. The colorist would often finish with clear varnish (gum arabic) to heighten colors.

HINGE: interior joining of the covers to the text block, the gutter formed by the pastedown and the front free endpaper.

IMPRINT: statement of place, publisher and date of publication on a book's title page.

INCUNABLE: from the cradle of printing, i.e., any book printed before 1500.

INSCRIBED: with an inscription (usually though not necessarily signed) by the author.

ISSUE: noted variation in a book's text, illustrations, binding or dust jacket intentionally made by the publisher—usually after publication. Various issues are treated as separate units for distribution to the trade. *"First issue"* precedes any such alterations or change.

LAID IN: paper or other material loosely inserted into a book.

LETTER SIGNED (LS): letter in a secretarial hand to which the author has added his or her own signature.

LITHOGRAPH: illustration produced by transferring an image drawn on stone to paper. The process allowed illustrations to more closely resemble the original drawings, paintings or sketches as it gave the lithographer a freedom of line impossible to achieve using a graver on a plate of copper or steel. Does not require the same sort of pressure as an engraving to transfer the image, but still has to be printed on separate stock from the text, usually by a printing house specializing in lithography. Also allows for the possibility of printing in color, adding another stone for each additional color desired (see *chromolithograph)*.

LIVRE D'ARTISTE (or artist's book): an example of a tradition of books illustrated with original hand-printed prints, usually issued in small editions on fine paper and often signed by the artist and author.

MANUSCRIPT SIGNED (MS): draft of a poem, play or work of prose, handwritten or typed, produced before publication though not necessarily as part of the publication process, and signed by the author.

MARGINALIA: handwritten notes made in the margins by a previous owner.

MISPAGINATED: printer's error in pagination, typically skipping, transposing or repeating page numbers. Not uncommon in older, larger books; printers assembled books using signatures and catchwords rather than page numbers. Not considered a defect, so long as all integral leaves are present, as all copies from a given print run would likely bear the same mistake.

MODERN: recently accomplished, when used to describe a book's binding that is not the original casing. Some books bound recently are bound using techniques, tools and styles of the period of the book's original issue; when done well this is called a *period-style binding*, a term that implies modern as well.

MOROCCO: binding material made from goatskin—versatile, durable, with a distinctive pebbled texture and visible grain. Readily stretched ("straight-grain"), crushed (flattened smooth), tooled in gilt or blind, inlaid with leathers of different colors. So-called because much of the raw material originally came from the tanneries of North Africa (other types of goatskin bindings denoting regions of origin include *levant, turkey, niger*).

OCTAVO (8vo): book composed of sheets printed on both sides, folded thrice, to make eight leaves and 16 pages. Typically between six and nine inches tall, more rectangular than square.

PLATE: full-page illustration printed separately from but bound with the text.

PERIOD-STYLE: binding executed with materials, tools and techniques to approximate the look of a contemporary binding from the period of the book's publication. The term implies that the binding is modern, or recent, unless otherwise specified (e.g., "nineteenth-century period-style calf" could describe a period-style binding executed in the nineteenth century covering a book printed much earlier).

POINT: variation in text, illustration, design or format that allows a bibliographer to distinguish between different editions and different printings of the same edition, or between different states or issues of the same printing.

PRESENTATION COPY: book given as a gift by its author, illustrator or publisher. Sometimes refers to a volume given by a notable donor.

PROVENANCE: history of a particular copy of a book.

QUARTO (4to): book composed of sheets printed on both sides, folded twice, to make four leaves and eight pages. Typically between nine and 14 inches tall, more square than rectangular.

REBACK: to supply a worn binding with a new spine, usually made of the same material as the rest of the binding and decorated to match. When feasible the binder may preserve the original spine and affix it to the new material, described as *"rebacked with the original spine laid down."*

SIGNED: with the signature of the author.

SIGNATURE: single sheet that has been printed on both sides and folded down to form the pages required by the book's format. A single signature of a quarto book, then, would be a sheet folded twice, containing four leaves, eight pages of text. Also called a *gathering* or a *quire*. Signatures are identified by a letter, symbol or number in the lower margin of the first page to make it easy for the printer to stack them in proper order for sewing.

STATE: noted variation in a book's text, illustrations, binding or dust jacket effected during the manufacturing process but for which no priority of issuance from the publisher can be determined. Sometimes a bibliographer can determine which state was produced first, but often the different states co-exist without any such determination. For example, if it is known that at some point during a print run a letter dropped from the forme, producing a typographical error, then copies with the correct text would be considered first-state and copies with the error second-state. However, all copies, regardless of state, would have been bound up and offered to the public on the same day.

TIPPED IN: leaf, plate or other paper neatly glued or otherwise attached to the text block.

TRADE EDITION: printing or printings of a book made available for purchase by the general public on publication day (as opposed to a *limited edition*, often available by subscription).

TYPED LETTER SIGNED (TLS): typewritten letter signed by the author.

UNCUT: edges of the text block (most apparent at the fore and lower edges) have not been trimmed to a uniform size, characterized by a ragged or *deckle edge*. A book may be uncut but opened—i.e., with a paper-knife—but all *unopened* books (see below) are by nature uncut as well. Considered quite desirable by most collectors.

UNOPENED: folds of a text block along the upper and fore-edges have not been trimmed away or opened with a paper-knife. While this makes it impossible to read all of the pages, it also indicates a probability that the text block has not been altered since leaving the printer.

VELLUM: binding material made from specially treated calfskin—durable, with a distinctive ivory color and smooth appearance. Can be tooled in gilt or blind. So-called *Japan vellum* (or Japon) is a type of thick paper that has been polished smooth and given a glossy finish to resemble vellum.

WOODCUT: illustration or textual decoration made by cutting away from the surface of a block of wood until the reverse of the image is left in relief; this is then inked and pressed to the paper to leave the image. The woodblock, or multiple blocks, can be fit into the forme along with the type, allowing text and illustrations to be printed in the same print run and share the same page, (not possible with *engravings*, which require thicker, damp paper and much more force; nor with *lithographs*, which require a different printing process altogether). Woodcuts preceded moveable type and are the earliest known printing technology.

WOOD-ENGRAVING: engraving made with the graver or burin on the cross-section of a piece of boxwood; the harder wood and finer tools allow for more delicate, finely detailed images, while the block can still be set in the forme alongside text and printed on the same stock as the text. The favored mode of book illustration of the latter half of the nineteenth century.

WORMHOLE: tiny pinhole-sized trails left by bookworms as they eat through a text block; much more common in older books printed on handmade papers with a high rag content than in books printed on manufactured papers made from wood pulp with a higher acidic content.

WRAPPERS: paper coverings, plain, marbled or printed, attached by stitches, staples or glue to a text block to identify it and afford it some protection (though much more fragile than a binding in plain, cloth- or leather-covered boards). More typical of slim volumes such as pamphlets. *Self-wrappers* are leaves, blank or printed, that are integral to the text block, conjugate with other leaves and from the same stock. *Original wrappers,* those attached at the time of issue, are scarce and extremely desirable to most collectors.

Acknowledgements

We would like to thank all the members of the staff of Bauman Rare Books who contributed to the creation of this book. Special thanks go to Corinne Weeks, Jessica Caum and Andy Hallman, as well as Jennifer Mercer, Zilpah Feiser, Michael Poteet, Heather O'Donnell and Niamh O'Connell. And thanks to Stephen Coan, who did the majority of the photographs featured in this guide for us over the past eighteen years.

Cover calligraphy by Harriet Rose Calligraphy.

Illustration Credits

We would like to thank the following sources for granting us permission to publish copyright images.

Thomas Moran (American, 1837-1926). Detail from *Grand Canyon of Arizona from Hermit Rim Road*, c. 1912. Color lithograph; 80.6 x 106 cm. © The Cleveland Museum of Art, Gift of Dr. Gerard and Phyllis Seltzer in honor of Phyllis Stone 1996.305.

Jacket cover for first edition of THE GREAT GATSBY by F. Scott Fitzgerald (New York: Scribner, 1925). Reprinted with permission of Scribner, an imprint of Simon & Schuster Adult Publishing Group.

Salvador Dalí, "The White Rabbit," from *Alice's Adventures in Wonderland* © 2006 Salvador Dalí, Gala-Salvador Dalí Foundation/Artists Rights Society (ARS), New York.

Henri Matisse, "Illustration for Ulysses," 1935. © 2006 Succession H. Matisse, Paris / Artists Rights Society (ARS), New York.

From THE CAT IN THE HAT by Dr. Seuss, copyright TM and copyright © by Dr. Seuss Enterprises, L. P. 1957, renewed 1985. Used by permission of Random House Children's Books, a division of Random House, Inc.

Jacket cover for first edition of A FAREWELL TO ARMS by Ernest Hemingway (New York: Scribner, 1929). Reprinted with permission of Scribner, an imprint of Simon & Schuster Adult Publishing Group.

Jacket cover for first edition of TENDER IS THE NIGHT by F. Scott Fitzgerald (New York: Scribner, 1934). Reprinted with permission of Scribner, an imprint of Simon & Schuster Adult Publishing Group.

Inscription by F. Scott Fitzgerald in first edition of *Tender is the Night* reproduced by permission of Harold Ober Associates, Inc.

First JB Lipincott edition BOOK COVER (1960) from TO KILL A MOCKINGBIRD by HARPER LEE. Copyright © 1960 by Harper Lee; renewed © 1988 by Harper Lee. Foreword copyright © 1993 by Harper Lee. Reprinted by permission of HarperCollins Publishers.

About the Authors

David and Natalie Bauman founded Bauman Rare Books in 1973. Today the company is among the largest and best known in the nation, with galleries on Madison Avenue in New York and in Philadelphia. Bauman Rare Books offers an extraordinary and extensive selection of rare books and autographs ranging from the fifteenth through the twentieth centuries. Having formed many important book collections through the years, the company is known for its meticulous research, exceptional inventory and large expert staff.